The Parables
of Jesus

Crossways International

Minneapolis, MN

My thanks go to Dr. Kenneth Bailey, scholar and friend, whom I have known since 1970, for permitting me to make use of his remarkable insights into Middle Eastern culture. I have long wanted to share his findings with people around the world.

THE PARABLES OF JESUS
was developed and written by
Harry Wendt, Minneapolis, MN

Illustrations by Knarelle Beard, Adelaide, South Australia

The Bible text in this publication is from the New Revised Standard Version of the Bible, copyrighted 1989 by the Division of Christian Education, National Council of Churches, New York, NY, and used by permission.

THE PARABLES OF JESUS
is published and distributed by
CROSSWAYS INTERNATIONAL
7930 Computer Avenue South
Minneapolis, MN 55435

Foreword

One of the most significant events of my life took place in Fall 1970, while I was doing graduate work in St. Louis: Dr. Ken Bailey and his family moved into the apartment next to the one in which my family and I were living. During the year that followed, Dr. Bailey and I talked frequently, and we have kept in touch ever since.

Prior to retirement, Dr. Bailey served as a professor of New Testament studies at Protestant and Catholic seminaries in Egypt, Lebanon, Jerusalem and Cyprus. Though he has written many articles for theological journals, he is best known for his four books on the parables of Jesus. The first of these is now out of print, but the latter three are still available. They are *Poet and Peasant* and *Through Peasant Eyes*, Grand Rapids: Eerdmans, 1976 and 1980 (printed in a combined edition, 1983); *Finding the Lost*, St. Louis: Concordia (1992). Pastors and teachers wishing to teach this study course would do well to purchase these volumes, the combined edition in particular.

Dr. Bailey emphasizes that we need to know something about the Middle Eastern culture to understand Jesus' parables. To read Bailey's writings is to be rapidly convinced of his position!

I am grateful to my colleague and friend for permitting me to draw on his knowledge to produce this study course. I am also most grateful to my fellow Australian, Knarelle Beard, who has worked with me for many years since we first met in 1977. Her illustrations in Crossways International's study manuals are used around the world. I hope you will be as delighted as I am with the sixteen illustrations she has produced for this publication.

I have shared Dr. Bailey's explanation of the parable of the Two Lost Sons with thousands of people around the world, and I have seen the impact it has made on their hearts. I trust the insights you'll read about in the pages ahead will touch you in a similar manner.

Harry Wendt

Harry Wendt

Contents

Note: Color transparencies of all illustrations in this volume are available from Crossways International.

Also by Dr. Wendt and available from Crossways International:*

- **Tell-Tale Timeline** ~ A vivid journey through the Bible in pictures and words.

- *The Bible's Big Story* (with time line) ~ Want to know your Bible but get stuck in Leviticus or Lamentations? We can help! Companion commentary to the Tell-Tale Timeline.

- *Road to Coronation* ~ Walk with Jesus on His way to the cross.

- *Christmas: The Real Story* ~ What really happened the first Christmas night in Bethlehem.

- *In Heaven's Name, Why on Earth?* ~ Christian living in the material world.

- *An Apostle's Creed for the New Millennium* ~ You'll confess ancient truths with fresh insight.

Other Bible surveys available from Crossways International:

- *Crossways* ~ Take a guided tour through the Bible with many interesting stops along the way.

- *The Divine Drama* ~ Looking for the Bible's big picture? This study will help you put the puzzling pieces together.

- *See Through the Scriptures* ~ Enjoy an "aha" experience with this short, captivating Bible survey.

The Fox, the Funeral, the Farewell, the Furrow

Luke 9:57–62

Introduction

1. Jesus faced constant political pressure and danger as He carried out His ministry. He resisted any move to make him an earthly king. Though He came to establish a kingdom, that kingdom was completely different from anything the world could devise or establish.

2. In Jesus' day, Galilee was ruled by Herod the Great's brutal son, Herod Antipas. There is reason to believe that Jesus used Capernaum (in the far northeast of Galilee) as a base for His ministry so that, when necessary, He could readily slip across the Jordan into the territory of Philip (another of Herod the Great's sons), who was much more moderate than Herod Antipas and much less likely to do Him physical harm.

3. Luke 9:51 reads:

   > When the days drew near for Jesus to be received up, he set his face to go to Jerusalem.

   This verse marks a geographical turning point in Jesus' ministry. Jesus was born in Bethlehem, five miles south of Jerusalem. He was presented in the Jerusalem Temple when eight days old. Joseph and Mary regularly took Him to Jerusalem for the annual Passover observance (Luke 2:41). Even so, Jesus kept away from Jerusalem during His ministry. If anything, Jerusalem played the role of the city of opposition to Jesus, the city of His enemies. Its political and religious leaders were opposed to His Person and ministry, and would eventually spearhead the move to do away with Him. Hence, when Jesus set his face to go to Jerusalem, He knew that He was going to His death, Luke 13:33–35!

4. Jesus sent messengers on ahead to prepare the way for Him and the disciples. The messengers went first to a Samaritan village, 9:52. But the Samaritans would not receive Jesus because He was heading for Jerusalem, 9:53. They insisted that the only legitimate place for worship was Mt. Gerizim, while the Jews argued that the only legitimate place was Jerusalem. Even so, Jesus rejected any notion of punishing the Samaritans for their attitude, 9:54–56; see also John 4.

© H.N. Wendt

The Parable

Frame 1, Luke 9:57: As they were going along the road, someone said to Jesus, "I will follow you wherever you go."

In Luke 9:57–62, soon after Jesus sets out for Jerusalem, He encounters three men. The first offers to follow Jesus. Jesus calls the second to follow him. The third offers to follow Jesus—but with a certain proviso. The six verses describing the three encounters contain statements that initially mystify Western readers—who usually feel a certain sympathy for the second and third persons mentioned. The second person *seemingly* says he will follow Jesus, but his father has just died and he must attend to funeral arrangements prior to joining Jesus. The third person *seemingly* says that he will follow Jesus, but he would first like to take just a little time to say good-bye to his family. These seem to be reasonable requests. However, the apparent meaning is not the real meaning.

Frame 2, Luke 9:58: And Jesus said to him, "Foxes have holes, and birds of the air have nests; but the Son of Man has nowhere to lay His head."

1. The first person, a volunteer, expresses a willingness to follow Jesus and go anywhere with Him, but has not considered the cost. His understanding of what is involved is shallow. Jesus might well have said to him:

    > It is easy to make big promises, if you think that only little is involved. You say you will go with me wherever I go? Good! But you must understand that I can offer you no salary, no benefits package and no retirement plan. I myself do not even own a bed to sleep on—and I cannot promise you one either. What goes for me must go for you as well!

2. But Jesus does not say that. Rather, He answers with remarkable but powerful brevity:

    > Foxes have dens.
    > Birds have roosts.
    > But the Son of Man has nowhere to lay his head.

3. Jesus uses verbal symbols in this passage—and with good reason. Still today, captive people cannot speak openly but must resort to verbal symbols. The people in Palestine in Jesus' day needed no reminders to do this; the memory of Roman and Herodian terror remained ever fresh in their minds. No one in his right mind dared openly criticize the Romans or Herodians, for their spies were everywhere.

4. The term "fox" was a symbol of the Ammonites, who were related to the Israelites, but were looked on as enemies. Similarly, the family of Herod the Great (Idumeans, descendants of the Edomites) was a racially mixed one. First century Palestinians would have understood the implications of Jesus' comment very well. In Luke 13:32, Jesus refers to Herod Antipas as "that fox."

5. "Birds have roosts" is a more appropriate translation than "birds have nests," for while birds have nests for only part of the year, they have roosts throughout the year. Furthermore, "birds of the air" is used in intertestamental literature as a term for the Gentile nations.

6. The sense of the saying may be: "Everybody is at home in Israel's land except the true Israel. The birds of the air (the Roman overlords) and the foxes (the Edomite interlopers) hold power and exercise

control. The true Israel is disinherited by them. If you throw in your lot with me, you join the ranks of the dispossessed, and you must be prepared to serve God under these conditions."

7. The call to follow a rejected, suffering Son of Man would have come as a shock to a first century Jew. After all, Daniel 7 contains no reference to suffering and hardship. It assured the Jewish people ("the saints of the Most High") that they would soon attain ascendancy over the nations of the world, and be served by those nations.

8. We might sum up the general thrust of Jesus' statement to this first candidate for discipleship as follows:

> If you want power and influence, follow the fox who manages his affairs with cunning. Go to the birds who feather their nests. Do you really want to follow the rejected Son of Man?

9. We are not told the young man's response. In every age there are those who glibly commit themselves to follow Jesus without seriously reflecting on the price people must pay for following a suffering, rejected Lord.

Frame 3, Luke 9:59,60: To another he said, "Follow me." But he said, "Lord, first let me go and bury my father." But Jesus said to him, "Let the dead bury their own dead; but as for you, go and proclaim the kingdom of God."

---

1. The second person does not offer his services to Jesus. Rather, Jesus seeks to recruit him with "Follow me." The tense of the verb Jesus uses (in the original language) in recruiting him suggests: "Start a new action! Get involved with Me full time!"

2. The man responds, "Lord, let me first go and bury my father." The response is often misunderstood. Some think the father has just died or is about to die, and the man is seeking just a little time to attend to his burial. This is not what is meant. If it were so, even from a common sense point of view, we would have to ask: "If his father has recently died, why is he not at home taking care of family affairs and funeral matters then and there?"

3. What the man really says is: "Let me go and serve my father while he is alive. After he dies I will bury him—and then I will come." He wants to defer following Jesus to a future time when his father will die as an old man—who knows when? Little does he know that in a very short time Jesus himself will give up His spirit!

4. This man's response reflects an attitude that still prevails today in the Middle East: A son has the duty to remain at home until his parents die. Then, and only then, can he consider other options. What is at stake here is peer pressure. The man's response to Jesus amounts to this: "Surely you do not expect me to violate the expectations of my community?"

Frame 4, Luke 9:61: Another said, "I will follow you, Lord; but let me first say farewell to those at home."

---

1. Though this would-be disciple rather brashly offers to follow Jesus, he has a precondition. On first hearing, the request seems legitimate enough. Who would not want to say good-bye to loved ones prior

4

to taking up some new career, some new mission in life? But this is not the issue. His request implies getting family permission.

2. Again, across the Middle East still today, the one who leaves asks permission to go. For example, an engineer in his forties will go from his large city to his village birthplace to get his father's permission to undertake foreign travel, a job change or a business venture. Though the granting of permission may be ceremonial and the son runs his own life, a sign of respect is involved. So the engineer poses his question and adds, "With your permission." His father grants permission with responses such as: "May you go in safety. May you go in peace. God go with you!" Little wonder, then, that many in the Middle East experience a degree of shock when they learn that Jesus' claim on people supersedes the claim of family— and that Jesus made this claim on people *when He was only about thirty*!

3. The one who wants to greet his family has his heart tied to his family—where the authority of the father is supreme. The man is saying, "I will follow you, Lord, but the authority of my father is higher than your authority. I must have his permission before I venture out!" Everyone listening knows that the father will refuse the son permission to wander off on some questionable enterprise.

Frame 5, Luke 9:62: Jesus said to him, "No one who puts a hand to the plow and looks back is fit for the kingdom of God."

---

1. Jesus draws on farming practices in the Palestine of His day in responding to the third individual. Then, as now, the plow is of light construction. The plowman uses his left hand to hold the plow, to regulate the depth of cut, and to lift it over rocks and stones. With his right hand, he directs his unruly ox out front, using a six-foot goad tipped with an iron spike. He must also look between the hindquarters of the ox to make sure that the furrow he is plowing will be straight. If he lets himself be distracted and looks around or behind himself, the result will be a crooked furrow.

2. In the Middle East, getting seed into the ground involves four plowings. In the *first*, big furrows are made to break up the soil. In the *second*, smaller furrows are made to provide proper drainage. In the *third*, close set furrows are plowed, without intervening bands. The seed is then sown. In the *fourth*, the seed sown by hand is covered.

3. Obviously, if the plowman is to carry out this sequence properly, he must give his undivided attention to the task at hand. If he lets himself get distracted, the plow might catch on a rock and cause the ox to expend a lot of unnecessary energy—and perhaps break the plow's point in the process. Distraction might also result in plowing previously plowed soil and destroying the field's drainage system or its potential to absorb water. It might also result in newly planted seed being left exposed to birds.

The Point of the Parable

1. The Talmud states that a father and his son, or a master and his disciple, are regarded as one individual. The issue at stake in the trio of encounters is the nature of the relationship that Jesus wants to exist between Himself as Master and Teacher, and His disciples and students. Jesus insists that loyalty to His Kingdom and its all-consuming demands supersede all other loyalties, including loyalty to family.

2. Becoming a disciple of Jesus is not "signing up for the course" to get a little information. It is the cementing of a lifelong relationship to a Person. Jesus' authority takes precedence over all relationships. The person who always wants to look back over the shoulder to check on family or other whims is judged of little value in the kingdom of God.

In "The Outline of History" (Vol. 1, pp. 425, 426), H.G. Wells summarizes the life of Jesus as he saw it outlined in the Gospels:

> Jesus was too great for His disciples. And in view of what He said, is it any wonder that all who were rich and prosperous felt a horror of strange things, a swimming of their world at His teaching? Perhaps the priests and rulers and rich men understood Him better than His followers. He was dragging out all the little private reservations they had made from social service into the light of a universal religious life. He was like a terrible moral huntsman, digging mankind out of the snug burrows in which they had lived hitherto. In the white blaze of His kingdom there was to be no property, no privilege, no pride, and no precedence, no motive and reward but love. Is it any wonder that men were dazzled and blinded, and cried out against Him? Even His disciples cried out when He would not spare them that light. Is it any wonder that the priests realized that between this Man and themselves there was no choice but that He or their priestcraft should perish? Is it any wonder that the Roman soldiers, confronted and amazed by something soaring over their comprehension and threatening all their disciplines, should take refuge in wild laughter, and crown Him with thorns, and robe Him in purple, and make a mock Caesar of Him? For to take Him seriously was to enter into a strange and alarming life, to abandon habits, to control instincts and impulses, to essay an incredible happiness... Is it any wonder that to this day this Galilean is too much for our small hearts?

Wells' statement describes vividly the challenge that Jesus poses still today for those who claim allegiance to Him.

The Good Samaritan

Luke 10:25–37

Jesus and Sirach

To understand the impact that Jesus' parable of the Good Samaritan would have had on His hearers, it is helpful to be familiar with (apocryphal) Sirach 12:1–7:

> If you do good, know to whom you do it,
>   and you will be thanked for your good deeds.
> Do good to the devout, and you will be repaid—
>   if not by them, certainly by the Most High.
> No good comes to one who persists in evil
>   or to one who does not give alms.
> Give to the devout, but *do not help the sinner.*
> Do good to the humble, but *do not give to the ungodly*;
>   *hold back their bread, and do not give it to them,*
>   for by means of it they might subdue you;
> then you will receive twice as much evil
>   for all the good you have done to them.
> For *the Most High also hates sinners*
>   *and will inflict punishment on the ungodly.*
> Give to the one who is good, but *do not help the sinner.*

The italicized sections draw attention to sentiments that Jesus rejected.

The Dialogue that Frames the Parable

The parable of the Good Samaritan is sandwiched between a theological dialogue. The parable itself is long, while the dialogue on either side of it is short. To understand the parable, we must understand the dialogue that brackets it. To ignore the dialogue is to reduce the parable to an exhortation to reach out to those in need. Unfortunately, Jesus' remarkable story has often been understood this way. The dialogue between Jesus and the lawyer is made up of eight speeches that fall into two rounds of debate.

1. In each round, there are two questions and two answers.

2. In each case, the lawyer asks the first question; Jesus does not answer the lawyer, but poses another question that the lawyer answers.

3. Each round closes with Jesus offering an answer to the original question.

4. Each round focuses on *doing* something to inherit eternal life.

5. Each round is introduced with words analyzing the motives of the lawyer: *first*, he wants to test Jesus; s*econd*, he wants to justify himself.

6. Each round ends with instructions about what to do.

The Opening Dialogue

Frame 1, Luke 10:25–29: *²⁵Just then a lawyer stood up to test Jesus. "Teacher," he said, "what must I do to inherit eternal life?" ²⁶He said to him, "What is written in the law? What do you read there?" ²⁷He answered, "You shall love the Lord your God with all your heart, and with all your soul, and with all your strength, and with all your mind; and your neighbor as yourself." ²⁸And he said to him, "You have given the right answer; do this, and you will live." ²⁹But wanting to justify himself, he asked Jesus, "And who is my neighbor?"*

---

1. *Speech 1, 10:25:* A lawyer poses a question to Jesus. He stands up when doing so—a social courtesy designed to show respect. At the same time, his goal is to "test" Jesus, indicating that there is something hypocritical about his actions.

2. The lawyer asks, "What shall I do to inherit eternal life?" We might ask: What can anyone *do* to *inherit* eternal life? People receive an inheritance as a gift, not as a reward for some performance. However, the word does have an Old Testament background in that Israel understood itself as inheriting the land of promise, even though they received it as a gift from God and had done nothing to deserve it.

3. In the postexilic period, the rabbis interpreted "to inherit the land" in terms of taking part in the "age to come." The inheritance becomes "eternal life," and the way to achieve that is to keep the law. Rabbi Hillel said that those who gain for themselves words of Torah have gained for themselves the life of the world to come. (*Torah*: The term could be used of the Pentateuch, or the law codes in the Pentateuch, or of the entire Old Testament.) An anonymous rabbinical saying reads, "Great is Torah, for it gives to them that practice it, life in this world and in the world to come."

4. In another noncanonical book, Slavonic Enoch, we read in ch. 9:

> This place [Eden], O Enoch, is prepared for the righteous, who endure all
> manner of offense from those that exasperate their souls, who avert their eyes
> from iniquity, and make righteous judgments, and give bread to the hungering,
> and cover the naked with clothing, and raise up the fallen, and help injured
> orphans, and who walk without fault before the face of the Lord, and serve him
> alone, and for them is prepared this place for eternal inheritance.

5. Possibly the rabbi expected Jesus to offer him a similar list of "dos and don'ts" that he and others might in turn debate with Jesus. Possibly, he suspected that, though some rabbis said that eternal life was achieved through keeping the law, Jesus was denying this teaching—a disturbing notion indeed!

6. *Speech 2, 10:26:* Jesus does not answer the question, but gets the lawyer to answer it himself. He asks the lawyer, "What is written in the law? What do you read there?"

7. *Speech 3, 10:27:* When Jesus probes the lawyer about what is in the law, the lawyer answers with a standard creed. He quotes and joins Deuteronomy 6:5 and Leviticus 19:18. Some say these two passages had already been joined by Jesus' day; others deny this. If the link had been made by Jesus' day, Jesus endorses it.

8. *Speech 4, 10:28:* The man can give the right answer, but does he act on it? In effect, the lawyer asks, "What, *having done*, will I inherit?" Jesus says, "*Keep on doing*"—a present imperative! He tells the lawyer, "If you want to inherit eternal life by your actions, just continually love God and your neighbor with the totality of all that you are." No line is drawn, and no list given; the requirements are limitless!

9. *Speech 5, 10:29:* The lawyer does not give up on the hope that he can earn his own entrance into eternal life. The law has been quoted; he needs some commentary. The God whom he must love is known. But who is this neighbor whom he must love as himself? He needs a definition, a list. So he initiates the next round of the debate.

10. He still hopes to do something to gain eternal life. He does not know mercy. He lives by his intention and ability to present himself as a righteous man before God. He wants to see himself as fully righteous. So he asks, "Who is my neighbor?" If Jesus answers, "Your relatives and friends," he can respond, "I have fully loved these." Then Jesus will praise him and say, "You have fully kept the law." The lawyer can then depart, accepting praise for his good works and enjoying a newly won honor and confidence.

11. The lawyer asked his question in a world that held a variety of views on precisely who the neighbor was. Leviticus identified the neighbor as the son of your own people, 19:17–19. Though the rabbis taught that all Jews should regard their fellow Jews as neighbors, they were divided over how to classify proselytes and were sure that Gentiles were not to be classified as neighbors. A *Midrash* (Jewish commentary) on Ruth reads:

> The Gentiles, amongst whom and us there is no war, and so those that are keepers of sheep amongst the Israelites, and the like, we are not to contrive their death; but if they be in any danger of death, we are not bound to deliver them; e.g., if any of them fall into the sea you shall not need to take them out; for it is said, "Thou shalt not rise up against the blood of thy neighbor"; but such a one is not thy neighbor.

12. The lawyer asks, "And who is my neighbor?" Jesus does not respond with a direct statement. Instead, He answers with a story—and, after telling the story, throws another question at the lawyer, "Which of these three, *do you think*, was a neighbor to the man who fell into the hands of robbers?"

13. In the parable, the robbers, the priest and the Levite come, do something and leave. The pattern is broken by the Samaritan who comes, does something, but does not leave. Seven statements describe the action of the Samaritan toward the wounded man. The list is long, for the Samaritan must make up for the omissions of the others.

The Parable, 10:30–35

Frame 2, Luke 10:30a: Jesus replied, "A man was going from Jerusalem to Jericho, and fell into the hands of robbers.

Many have noted that the 17-mile descent from Jerusalem to Jericho has been dangerous throughout history. The crusaders built a small fort at the halfway mark to protect pilgrims.

Frame 3, Luke 10:30b: Who stripped him, beat him, and went away, leaving him half dead.

---

1. The robbers take the victim's money and leave him half dead, with no thought of returning. The term "half dead" implies "next to dead."

2. No description is given of the victim, but logic suggests he is a Jew. Though in the world of that day there were many ethnic groups, it was possible to identify people's roots by their speech and dress. But this victim is robbed of his clothes and is unable to speak. Those who stumble across him on the road do not know who he is, and have no way of finding out.

Frame 4, Luke 10:31: Now by chance, a priest was going down on that road; and when he saw him, he passed by on the other side.

---

1. Because priests were among the upper class, it is likely the priest in the parable is riding a donkey. People do not hike 17 miles through the desert—unless they have to. Money determines the manner: The poor walk; the rich ride.

2. The priest finds himself faced with a dilemma: How does he know the victim is a neighbor? Because the robbers took the victim's clothes, the priest cannot determine his ethnic roots. Because the victim is unable to speak, he cannot identify him by his accent. Why, the man might even be a non-Jew!

3. Another possibility exists: The man might even be dead—and if he is, the priest dare not touch him. To touch a Gentile or a dead Jew would defile him. As a priest, he cannot go closer than four cubits to a corpse. He would have to overstep that boundary just to determine the condition of the victim. If he does that, and the victim is indeed dead, the priest will have to rend his garments.

4. More: The priest collects, distributes and eats tithes. If he defiles himself by touching a "prohibited" person or body, he can do none of these things. His family and his servants will also suffer the consequences! So, perhaps the priest rides by, sees the victim, looks at him haughtily, crosses over the road to distance himself from him—and continues on his way! Indeed, his family might well have applauded him for his course of action. After all, he has wisely avoided any inconvenience to himself and any loss to his family.

5. Levites gave priests a "tithe of the tithe"—for them and their household to eat. This could only take place when the recipient was in a state of ritual purity. While under a ban of defilement, he could not wear phylacteries or officiate at any service. The law specified five sources of defilement, two of which were to touch a dead body and to have contact with a non-Jew.

6. Many priests served for two-week periods in Jerusalem but lived in Jericho. Because ritual purification could take place only in the Jerusalem Temple, the priest would have to return there if he

became defiled. The process of restoring purity was costly, humiliating and time-consuming; a week was required! Among other things, the process involved finding and buying a red heifer, and reducing it to ashes.

7. The priest might rationalize his actions by presuming that, after all, the victim is a sinner or a Gentile—and help offered to sinners might be viewed as a labor against God who detests sinners.

Frame 5, Luke 10:32: So likewise a Levite, when he came to the place and saw him, passed by on the other side.

---

1. Still today in many parts of the world, travelers are often very interested in who else is on the road; their life might depend on it. Hence, to get information, they exchange a few words in a village before entering a desert. They look for glimpses of anyone traveling ahead of them, and exchange comments with travelers coming toward them. They keep their eyes open for any fresh tracks of people or animals.

2. The traces of the old Roman road from Jerusalem to Jericho are still visible. In Jesus' day, those traveling on it were able to see the road ahead for a considerable distance. Middle Eastern people assume the Levite knew the priest was ahead of him.

3. A Levite was not bound by as many regulations as a priest. He was only required to observe ritual cleanliness in the course of his cultic activities. Had he set out to provide the victim with aid and found the man to be dead, the consequences would have been less serious for him. But, as with the priest, because the victim cannot talk, the Levite cannot find out if the victim is his neighbor. The priest saw and passed by. The Levite comes to the place, sees and passes by.

4. Because the Levite was from a poorer, lower social class, most likely he was walking. He might have gone quite close to the victim, even crossed the "defilement line" out of curiosity, then decided against offering aid and kept going. For him, fear of defilement might not have been the issue; the fear of being robbed might have been. Yes, he could have rendered first aid—but to stay meant risk from robbers.

5. Perhaps he did not want to show up the priest's lack of compassion. Perhaps he did not want to act contrary to the priest's interpretation of the Law! Perhaps he might have rationalized things by asking himself, "If the priest did nothing, why should I act differently?" The command not to defile was unconditional. The command to serve the neighbor was conditional.

6. In a very real way, the priest and the Levite were victims of an evil system. The scribes met constantly to bring the traditions up-to-date to meet new situations. Life was a codified "do" and "do not." The practice persists widely today.

Frame 6, Luke 10:33,34a: But a Samaritan while traveling came near him; and when he saw him, he was moved with pity. He went to him and bandaged his wounds, having poured oil and wine on them.

---

1. The priest goes down the road. The Levite comes to the place. The Samaritan comes to the man. The Samaritan, too, risks contamination—which extends to his animals and his wares. He, too, is a prime target for robbers—who might have respected the priest and Levite, but would not have respected a Samaritan!

2. The priest could have taken the victim to safety by donkey—but did not. The Levite could have rendered first aid—but did not. Most likely the Samaritan knows the priest and Levite passed him by, and he might even have been traveling uphill. He could have argued, "They did not help; why should I?"—but he did not!

3. He has a strong gut-level reaction to the wounded man. Though he himself is a Samaritan and not a Jew, he is bound by the same Torah—which tells him that "neighbor" is countryman and kinsman. Because he is traveling in Judah, it is less likely that any victim is a neighbor. Even so, the Samaritan is the one who acts.

4. He cleans and softens the wounds with oil, disinfects them with wine, and then binds them up. (The Old Testament scriptures often speak of God binding up the wounds of His stricken people.)

5. The Samaritan is the one who pours out the true offering acceptable to God. Oil and wine were used as sacramental elements in Temple worship. The term "pour" is from the language of worship, and had to do with libations in connection with sacrifices. Though the Samaritan apparently understands true worship, the priest and the Levite do not! See Hosea 6:6; Micah 6:1–8.

6. That a Samaritan should help a Jew is all the more remarkable in the light of Sirach, 50:25–26:

> Two nations my soul detests,
>   and the third is not even a people.
> Those who live in Seir, and the Philistines,
>   and the foolish people that live in Shechem.

Note: Seir was the chief mountain range in Edom, Shechem the "home city" for the Samaritans.

The passage groups the Samaritans with Philistines and Edomites. Worse yet, the Mishnah (a Jewish commentary on the law) stated, "He that eats the bread of Samaritans is like one that eats the bread of swine." The Jews publicly cursed the Samaritans in their synagogues, and prayed daily that the Samaritans might not be partakers of eternal life. The feelings of animosity were mutual, for numerous reasons. Josephus tells us that, some years prior to Jesus' ministry, the Samaritans had defiled the Temple by scattering human bones in the Temple court. Heretics and schismatics were hated more than unbelievers!

Frame 7, Luke 10:34b: Then he put him on his own animal.

---

1. When the Samaritan appears, the text implies that he is riding. Had he been walking (like the Levite), he could have rendered first aid, but no more. Because he is riding, he can do more than render first aid; he can do what the priest should have done!

2. Most likely the Samaritan has other animals, but puts the victim on his own.

3. In the Middle East, donkeys can carry two people, and the role of riders and leaders of animals is crucial. Perhaps the Samaritan leads the animal. (Here we might note Esther 6:7–11, where Haman has to lead the horse on which Mordecai rides.) If so, a possibly well-to-do merchant assumes the role of a servant!

14

Frame 8, Luke 10:34b: He brought him to an inn, and took care of him.

1. The Samaritan acts bravely when he stops in the desert. He acts even more bravely when he carries out the final act of compassion!

2. If the wounded man regains consciousness, he may insult the Samaritan for his kindness, because oil and wine were considered forbidden objects if they emanated from a Samaritan. Not only have they come from someone considered unclean, but the tithe has not been paid on them—and by accepting them the wounded man incurs an obligation to pay tithes for them. But he has recently been robbed and obviously has no way even to pay the hotel bill. The Pharisees would have been pleased if the wounded man had shouted, "Get away from me, you abomination! I will have none of your oil or your wine."

3. We must bear in mind that the law of retaliation is still alive and well in the Middle East. You may kill the killer, or any member of the killer's family or clan. If you bring a victim to a place for help, the locals may assume you caused the victim's injury. They may turn on you—especially if you are from a hated minority group.

4. The Samaritan might well have left the victim at the inn door and fled. But by staying with him and promising to return, there can be no anonymity for the Samaritan. Despite all the dangers and risks, the Samaritan takes the victim to the inn, remains with him overnight, and cares for him.

5. The Samaritan might have taken the man to the home of a relative or friend, even his own home. But for the sake of the point that the story sets out to make: Had the Samaritan done this, he could not have paid family or friends, and there would have been no point in returning if the final scene took place in the victim's village.

6. Innkeepers had a very unsavory reputation. The Mishnah stated:

    > Cattle may not be left in the inns of gentiles since they are suspected of bestiality;
    > nor may a woman remain with them since they are suspected of lewdness; nor
    > may a man remain with them since they are suspected of shedding blood.

    Jewish inns did not fare any better. Some Jewish rabbis used the term "prostitute" for a woman who keeps an inn.

*Frame 9, Luke 10:35: The next day he took out two denarii, gave them to the innkeeper, and said,
 'Take care of him; and when I come back, I will repay you whatever more you spend.'"*

1. The victim has no money left. If he has no money, he can be arrested for debt. If he cannot pay for his accommodation and care, he cannot leave the inn. But the Samaritan pays all expenses from his own pocket, leaves the victim provided for, and promises to return to pay whatever else might be owing. Thus he provides for the man's recovery and enables him to get out of town.

2. What the Samaritan did, the priest could have done, and should have done. He compensates even for the actions of the robbers. They robbed, deserted, abandoned. He pays, has the victim taken care of, and returns!

3. A Jew dealing with a Jew could have gotten his money back. A Samaritan dealing with a Jew has little hope. In going to the help of his Jewish neighbor, the Samaritan expends time, effort and money, and exposes himself to personal danger. We might add: Just like God!

The Closing Dialogue, 10:36, 37

Frame 10, Luke 10:36,37: [Jesus asked] "Which of these three, do you think, was a neighbor to the man who fell into the hands of the robbers?" He said, "The one who showed him mercy." Jesus said to him, "Go and do likewise."

---

1. The lawyer had asked Jesus, "And who is my neighbor?" Jesus rephrased and reversed the question into, "To whom must I be a neighbor?" In telling the parable, Jesus removed all limits as to who the neighbor is, and all limits as to how far His followers must go in serving that neighbor.

2. Jesus could have told a story about a noble Jew helping a hated Samaritan. It would have sounded good to his audience, and they would have remained emotionally absorbed. However, Jesus told a story that took considerable courage to tell—about a "hated" Samaritan who was morally superior to Jewish religious leadership. (After all, though the robbers caused hurt by violence, the religious leaders caused hurt by neglect!)

   Tragically, the lawyer does not recognize Jesus, the Good Samaritan, before him, nor his own need of Jesus' help!

The so-called Golden Rule exists in many of the world's major religions:

ISLAM: "None of you is a believer if he does not desire for his brother that which he desires for himself." (Sunna)

JUDAISM: "That which you hold as detestable, do not do to your neighbor. That is the whole law; the rest is but commentary." (Talmud, Sabbat, 31)

BRAHMANISM (Orthodox Hinduism): "Such is the sum of duty: do not do to others that which, to you, would do harm to yourself." (Mahabharata, 5, 1517)

BUDDHISM: "Injure not others in a manner that would injure you." (Udana-Varga, 5, 18)

CONFUCIANISM: "Here certainly is the golden maxim: Let us not do to others that which we do not want them to do to us." (Analects, 15, 23)

TAOISM: "Consider that your neighbor gains your gains and loses that which you lose." (Tai Shang Kan Ying Pian)

CHRISTIANITY: "In everything do to others as you would have them do to you." (Jesus in Matthew 7:12, NRSV)

A careful comparison reveals a significant truth. While the first statements call the faithful to refrain from *doing harm* to others, Jesus calls His followers to devote life to *doing good* to others! Furthermore, Jesus removed all limits as to who the neighbor is and how far one should go in serving that neighbor.

The Friend at Midnight

Luke 11:5–8

The Setting, 11:1–4

1. In Matthew 6:1–8, the background to the giving of the Lord's Prayer is as follows: Jesus warns His hearers against practicing their piety, and praying just to be seen, verses 1–6. He warns them against trying to manipulate God by using a multitude of words, verses 7,8. He then gives them the Lord's Prayer—as a guideline for prayer rather than as a prayer to be repeated *verbatim*.

2. In Luke 11:1–4, the situation is a little different. After the disciples observe Jesus at prayer, they ask Him to teach them to pray—just as John the Baptist taught his disciples to pray. Jesus responds by giving them the words of the Lord's Prayer—in a form that differs somewhat from that in Matthew. He then tells the disciples a parable to encourage them to pray with confidence and fervor.

The Parable, 11:5–8

1. The parable opens with a question expecting the answer, "No! Never!" The question Jesus puts to the disciples runs along these lines:

> A friend from a distant village comes to your home just before midnight, and you must provide him with a meal and accommodation. But you don't have the necessary items to feed him as you should. So you go to one of your neighbors to borrow some bread—and the neighbor offers ridiculous excuses about a locked door and sleeping children. Can any of you imagine that happening?

The Middle Easterner responds emphatically, "No, I cannot imagine such a thing! It could never happen!"

2. People in the Western World often misunderstand the meaning of the parable because of a mistranslation. English translations, for example, suggest that the "friend" eventually responds to the request because of the "importunity" (RSV) or "persistence" (NRSV) of the person making the request. These renditions of the key Greek word *aneideia* are influenced by the verses immediately following it. The meaning of the parable becomes clear when the cultural setting behind the story is properly understood, and *aneideia* is correctly translated.

© H.N. Wendt

3. The key issue at stake in the parable is *the avoidance of shame*. The NRSV translates the opening phrase, "Suppose." It should be translated, "Can any of you imagine...?" In Luke 11:5, Jesus is expecting a negative answer. He is asking, "Can you imagine going to a neighbor, asking for help to entertain a friend, and getting this kind of response?" The Oriental responsibility for a guest is legendary. The Oriental listener/reader cannot understand how anyone might offer excuses about a closed door and sleeping children when providing proper hospitality to a guest is at stake.

Frame 1, Luke 11:9,10,13: "⁹So I say to you, Ask, and it will be given you; search, and you will find; knock, and the door will be opened for you. ¹⁰For everyone who asks receives, and everyone who searches finds, and for everyone who knocks, the door will be opened....¹³If you, then, who are evil, know how to give good gifts to your children, how much more will the heavenly Father give the Holy Spirit to those who ask him!"

In Luke 11:1–4, when the disciples ask Jesus to teach them to pray, He teaches them the kind of things they should pray for and about, in the words of the Lord's prayer. In 11:5–8, Jesus tells a parable to assure his hearers that, when they pray, they pray to a loving heavenly Father who is more than ready and willing to hear them. In 11:9–13, He assures them that when they pray for the Holy Spirit (for faith in Jesus, and for his mind and manner), they will be given what they ask for. In frame 1, the mind and manner of Jesus is depicted in terms of a crowned servant figure, with basin and towel. The dove symbolizes the Holy Spirit.

Frame 2, Luke 11:5,6: And Jesus said to them, "Suppose one of you has a friend, and you go to him at midnight and say to him, 'Friend, lend me three loaves of bread; for a friend of mine has arrived, and I have nothing to set before him.'

---

1. A man has a friend arrive at his home in the late hours of the night. In the desert areas of Syria, Jordan and Egypt it is necessary to travel by night because of the heat. It is not customary to do so in Palestine and Lebanon because of the proximity of the sea and sea breezes. Thus, the arrival of a friend at midnight is unusual.

2. The friend's arrival creates a challenge for the host. He must set something before the guest, and the guest must eat—whether he is hungry or not. The host does not plan to set merely bread before his guest. He will also place before him a variety of items in dishes—and the guest will use the bread as his knife, fork and spoon. As he eats, he will break off bite-sized pieces of bread, dip them into the various dishes, and put a succession of "sops" into his mouth. The contents of the various dishes are never defiled from the eater's mouth because he begins each bite with a fresh piece of bread.

3. But he has no bread! He may have some "leftovers," but he cannot set them before his guest. To feed the guest with a partial loaf left over from a previous meal would be an insult. He must set unbroken loaves or pieces before him, and he must put before the guest more than he will eat.

Frame 3, Luke 11:7: And he answers from within, 'Do not bother me; the door has already been locked, and my children are with me in bed; and I cannot get up and give you anything.'

---

1. The situation is often understood as follows: The host goes to a neighbor's home, knocks at his door to get his attention, and calls out that he needs some bread to feed his guest. The neighbor initially ignores him and hopes he will go away. It is late! He wants to sleep! More, the door is bolted and his children are asleep! He does not want to have to mess with his neighbor! But the neighbor keeps on

knocking! So, finally, he responds: "The door is bolted. My children are in bed with me—and they are asleep. I can't help you at this hour of the night!"

2. However, the host does not persist in knocking, because he does not knock. A stranger knocks. A friend calls. When he calls, the neighbor will recognize the voice and not be frightened.

3. With regard to the door being bolted and the children being asleep: These are weak excuses. The door bolt is not heavy. Even if the children do stir, they will soon fall asleep again. These excuses are so unthinkable that they are humorous.

4. How does the host know to which house he should go to get the required bread? Still today in Palestinian villages, women cooperate in baking bread, and it is known who has baked recently. Obviously, the host's supplies are finished. The family's dough will be taken to the village oven the next morning. On the other hand, it appears that the sleeper's house has recently completed baking a batch of loaves—and this could be enough to last for a week or more.

5. Though the host initially asks for bread, everyone knows that he also needs to borrow the food that will be eaten with the bread. This becomes clear in verse 8, where the sleeper gives him whatever he needs. So, the host starts his round to gather up the greater portion of the meal from the neighbor, or various neighbors. He will also borrow the best tray, pitcher, cloth and goblets available.

6. Note the situation to this point: *First,* the host is a host and not a borrower. He is not asking for anything for himself. *Second,* he goes to one friend to honor a second friend. *Third,* he is asking for the food of bare subsistence.

Frame 4, Luke 11:8: I tell you, even though he will not get up and give him anything because he is his friend, at least because of his persistence [better, "sense of shame"; see below] he will get up and give him whatever he needs.

---

1. The verse is traditionally understood to mean that because the host persists relentlessly with his knocking, the neighbor finally succumbs and grants his request.

2. However, suggestions that the "friend" responded because of the host's "importunity" or "persistence" miss the point, and are misleading translations. The word used should be translated as "sense of shame," and the reference is to the man *inside,* not to the man *outside.* The emphasis on persistence may apply to other parables, but not to this one.

3. Westerners wishing to understand this parable must note that, in Palestine still today, a crucial element is that a guest is the guest of the *community,* not just of the *individual.* This is reflected in the language extended to the guest: "You have honored *our village*"—and never, "You have honored *me.*" Thus the community is considered responsible for hosting and entertaining a guest. A guest must leave the village with a good feeling about the hospitality of the village as a community. Because of the sense of close community in life in the Middle East, and because of the role that extending hospitality plays, borrowing there has been developed into a fine art.

4. The host is not a pauper. He himself has plenty of food: olives, grape-molasses, cheese—and a variety of other things. These are gathered and prepared and stored on a yearly basis. When the host says, "I have nothing to set before him" (11:6), he is speaking idiomatically and means, "I have nothing adequate to serve my guest so that the *honor of our village* will be upheld." Again the appeal to the community is the main point.

5. The neighbor acts, therefore, not necessarily for the sake of *friendship*, but for the sake of his *reputation*. He knows that the host must gather up the essentials for the banquet from the various neighbors. If he refuses the request of anything as humble as a loaf of bread, the host will continue on his rounds cursing the sleeper's stinginess for refusing to grant a trifling request. The story will be all over the village by morning. The sleeper will be met with cries of "Shame!" everywhere he goes. Because of his desire for "avoidance of shame" he will arise and provide whatever the borrower wants. In short, in going to his neighbor, the host is asking the sleeper to fulfill his duty to the guest of the village. As long as the request is modest enough, refusal is unthinkable.

6. Hence, the illustration depicts the parable's unfolding narrative when it is properly understood. The traveler goes on his way the next day, and all in the village turn out to bid him farewell. The host is there. The neighbor is there. Everyone is there. The traveler has been provided with food fitting the occasion, and a place to sleep. The village has honored its obligations. The host's reputation is intact. The neighbor's good name is preserved. Both have risen to the occasion.

Frame 5, Luke 11:11,12: Is there anyone among you who, if your child asks for bread, will give a stone; or if your child asks for a fish, will give a snake instead of a fish? Or if the child asks for an egg, will give a scorpion?"

---

1. This section is best understood as a separate unit and not as part of the previous story. Verse 11 is a parable composed of three comparisons. To understand it, we must bear in mind that in Palestine, bread, fish and eggs are the ordinary food of the common people. Furthermore, a round stone looks like a round loaf. There is little outward difference between the snake of the sea (eel, which is a kind of fish) and the snake of the land, which is an ordinary snake. A scorpion all folded up looks like an egg.

2. Travelers to Palestine in previous centuries spoke of a type of fish (*barbut*), then found in the Sea of Galilee, that could reach five feet in length, crawl on land, and had the appearance of a snake. It was classified among the unclean fish. It seems quite likely that this was the "snake" of the story. The fisherman's net would regularly catch both edible fish and the eel-like creature—and the latter would be cast back into the sea as unclean and non-edible. Hence, the meaning of 11:11 appears to be: "If a child asks a parent for a fish, will the parent give the child a 'snake' out of the sea?"

3. In short, Luke 11:9–13 teaches that, as a parent will always give a child gifts, and those gifts will be good, those who ask of God can be assured that God will give them even better gifts than those a parent gives a child! Note the following:

    a. In 11:1–8, a neighbor deals with a neighbor; in verse 11, a parent deals with a child.

    b. In 11:1–8, there is no one asking for something good and getting something bad; in this section, this is the burden of the imagery.

    c. In 11:1–8, there is no reference to persistence; in this section, continued action is implied: *Keep on* asking, seeking, knocking.

    d. In 11:1–8, a friend *calls* to his neighbor; here persistent *knocking* is introduced.

Summary

1. A situation can arise in going to a neighbor when everything is against you. It is night. He is in bed. The door is locked. The children are asleep. He is annoyed at being disturbed. Even so, you will receive even more than you ask! This is because your neighbor is a man of integrity and he will not violate that quality.

2. If you are confident of having your needs met when you go to such a neighbor in the night, how much more can you rest assured when you take your requests to a loving Father in heaven? The God to whom you pray also has an integrity that He will not violate—and beyond this, He loves you.

3. Luke 11:5–7 and 11:9–13 teach that God is a God of honor and that people can have complete assurance that their prayers to God will be heard. After all, the One to whom they pray is more than willing to listen to them, and to grant them the power and guidance of the Holy Spirit, 11:13 (*depicted in the central frame*). God's will for His children is that they learn to love and serve each other as God loves and serves them. Their Lord and Heavenly Brother, though the King of the universe, took upon Himself the form of a Servant and washed His disciples' feet. His brothers and sisters are to pray fervently that they might constantly reflect the mind and manner of Jesus in their lives.

In Matthew's account of the giving of the Lord's Prayer (6:9–13), Jesus gives His followers *guidelines* for prayer rather than a prayer that is to be prayed mechanically, word by word. Though Christians can approach God with every confidence, knowing that their prayers will be heard, they do well to note the things their Heavenly Brother, Jesus, wants them to pray about and for.

In praying "Our," they pray not only for their own needs, but for the needs of humanity around the world. The "Father in heaven" to whom they pray is not limited in power, nor subject to moods, as are earthly parents. More, God is the Maker and Owner of all things, and the one who supplies all needs (not greeds!). They pray that things on earth, and within their own lives, might be as they are in God's invisible but present and eternal realm ("on earth, as it is in heaven"). They pray that they might live to honor and reflect their Maker and Owner, rather than the realm of the demonic, the world and their flesh. They pray that they might know and submit to God as King, rather than buckle under to the whims of the demonic, the world and their flesh. They pray that they might know and do God's will, rather than submit to the will of the demonic, the world and their flesh. They pray that God would teach them to understand that God is the One who provides their needs— and that they should be grateful, and serve as God's instruments to supply the needs of others. As God forgives that God might go on serving them, they are to forgive others to remove all roadblocks to serving them. They pray that God will enlighten them to understand the testing that is present every step along the way—and enlighten and empower them to recognize and resist the "evil one" (Matthew 6:13, NRSV).

The Lord's Prayer is the Christian's "war cry." It is the "key signature" that guides all prayers and prayer requests. Those who understand it pray that they might live usefully rather than comfortably, and that their lives might reflect the spirit of Jesus rather than the spirit of the world around them.

The Rich Fool

Luke 12:13–21

Introduction

Luke says more about the downtrodden and poor than any other New Testament writer. His concern echoes that of Amos. At the same time, history reveals only too clearly that many people are more concerned with what is due to them rather than what is due to others. To grant people *their* understanding of *their* rights can lead to tragedy. Jesus stresses that people need to solve problems by developing a new understanding of themselves, Luke 13:1–3.

Opening Dialogue, 12:13–15

1. Throughout history, dividing an inheritance has always been a sensitive issue and has created countless problems. Psalm 133:1 meditates on how good it is when sons cooperate harmoniously in dealing with such situations; in the psalm, to "live together in unity" is a technical term.

2. The parable of the rich fool is preceded by an opening dialogue between Jesus and an anonymous petitioner. The petitioner makes a demand of Jesus, and Jesus responds to that demand. The issue at stake has to do with the age-old problem of dividing an inheritance. The dialogue gives rise to the parable that follows.

The Structure of the Parable, 12:16–21

1. There is one "wisdom saying" before the parable (12:15b), and another after it, 12:21. In between come five stanzas:

    a. In the first, goods are given.
    b. In the fifth, the same goods are left behind.
    c. In between, the rich man makes three speeches in which he discusses *with himself* ways of ensuring his future security. His goal is to enjoy the good life while life lasts. It is possible that these speeches reflect the sweep of time between recognizing and resolving the challenge.

2. The center stanza of the rich man's philosophizing constitutes the crucial turning point in the story: *he* determines what *he* will do to resolve what *he* sees to be the problem. *He* consults with a committee of one—*himself*! But God has the final say. What the *man* plans to do is one thing. What *God* plans to

do is another. The man spends his life accumulating and storing goods—only, finally, to be taken from them. He goes; the goods stay. In the closing section of the parable, the rich man learns that what he thought were *possessions* were *endowments*, and *even his soul is on loan from God!*

Ecclesiastes 5:10 makes a point that speaks to the passage as a whole: "The lover of money will not be satisfied with money; nor the lover of wealth, with gain."

Frame 1, Luke 12:13–15 (initial dialogue): Someone in the crowd said to Jesus, "Teacher, tell my brother to divide the family inheritance with me." But he said to him, "Friend, who set me to be a judge or arbitrator over you?" And he said to him, "Take care! Be on your guard against all kinds of greed; for one's life does not consist in the abundance of possessions."

---

1. Jesus' questioner *knows* what he wants, and tries to *use* Jesus to *get* what he wants. He does not *ask* Jesus for an opinion, but *orders* Jesus to implement a specific course of action. He wants Jesus to help him pressure his brother into finalizing the division *he has already decided on.*

2. In dealing with the issue of dividing an inheritance, *Roman law* required the agreement of both parties. *Jewish rabbis* taught that if one brother wanted a division, it should be granted. Rabbis were expected to know the law and give a legal ruling in keeping with it.

3. In the opening statement (12:13), the man addresses Jesus as "teacher" or "rabbi." Hence, the man is saying to Jesus, "You are a rabbi—and everyone knows the opinion of the rabbis. I am right and my brother is wrong. You tell him so!" The man who confronts Jesus has decided what *his* rights are. He wants Jesus to help him pressure his brother to grant those rights.

4. Little wonder, then, that Jesus' response has a note of gruffness to it: "Man, who set me to be a judge or arbitrator over you?" He refuses to act as a judge and divider, and rebuffs the petitioner. The relationship between the man and his brother is obviously already broken, and the man wants it finalized by total separation. But Jesus did not come to *divide* but to *reconcile*. He wants to bring people together, not separate them.

5. What the questioner needs is a new understanding of himself. He must learn that there is a greater gain than *getting* an inheritance, and a greater loss than *losing* an inheritance. *The petitioner's problems will not be resolved even if his brother does agree to divide.*

6. Hence, in what follows, Jesus becomes a judge *over* them—not *between* them. He judges their hearts, not their pocket books. Both brothers must learn that there is more to life on earth than physical life.

7. Jesus says, "Take care! Be on your guard against all kinds of greed," 12:15a. He follows this up with a wisdom statement: "One's life does not consist in the abundance of possessions," 12:15b.

The Parable

Frame 2, Luke 12:16,17 (the problem and the debate): Then Jesus told them a parable: "The land of a rich man produced abundantly. And he thought to himself, 'What should I do, for I have no place to store my crops?'

---

1. The parable begins with, "The land of a rich man produced abundantly," 12:16. But tragically, the man presumes that he owns himself, the land, and what the land produces.

2. We are not told how the rich man of the parable got his riches. He has enough and more than enough. Now he finds himself having to deal with another bumper crop. He did not earn it and he does not need it. But what is he to do with it?

3. "And he thought within himself, 'What should I do, for I have no place to store my crops?'" (12:17). The rich man debates within himself, perhaps for quite some time. He does not conclude that he is already sufficiently wealthy and does not need all this extra. He gives no thought to thanking God for the additional abundance. He simply refers to the bumper crops as "my crops," and his only concern is how to preserve them to benefit himself.

4. When considering where he will store his abundance, one thought eludes him. As the Church Father, Ambrose of Milan, pointed out, ample storage was already available—*in the mouths of the poor and needy*! (Note the onlookers and the poor in frames 2 and 3.) True, Paul says that we are to work so that we do not become a burden on others, 2 Thessalonians 2:7–12. However, he also states that we are to work to be in a position to minister to the needs of others, Ephesians 4:28.

Frame 3, Luke 12:18,19 (the solution and the goal): Then he said, 'I will do this: I will pull down my barns and build larger ones, and there I will store all my grain and my goods. And I will say to my soul, 'Soul, you have ample goods laid up for many years; relax, eat, drink, be merry.'

---

1. The decision is: "I will pull down my barns and build larger ones, and there I will store all my grain and my goods," 12:18.

2. Tragically, the possessive pronoun "my" shows up repeatedly throughout his deliberations with himself. He is alone when he makes his decision, and he will be alone when he consumes God's gifts (better, God's "endowments").

3. The man speaks to himself—not the community. This is remarkable, for in the Middle East people live in tightly knit communities. The leading men of the village still "sit at the gate" and spend literally years talking to one another. The smallest transaction gives rise to hours of discussion. But the rich man has no one with whom to discuss his concerns and trusts no one. His wealth is his personal prison. He, therefore, meets only with his committee of one, himself, and finally makes his decision.

4. At that time, tithes and offerings were set aside in barns, and priests and Levites collected them from there. However, the man does not place his goods in barns that priests and Levites might collect them; he stores them in a place where they will ensure an ongoing abundant life for himself, 12:19.

5. The rich man makes a speech, but it is tragic. He has a solution, but it is pitiful. He has no one to whom he can announce his solution—no village, family, friends, village elders, fellow landowners, or servants and their families.

   In the three parables of Luke 15, the shepherd, the woman and the father have others to whom they can announce good news and with whom they can celebrate. The rich man has nobody. When he addresses his "soul," he addresses his total person.

6. He says, "I will say to my soul, 'Soul, you have ample goods laid up for many years; relax, eat, drink, be merry.'" He thinks that the total needs of his total person can be met by material surpluses. He sees his little world existing for his own exclusive use and enjoyment. (*Note the martini in frame 3.*)

Frame 4, Luke 12:20 (death and dilemma): But God said to him, 'You fool! This very night your life is being demanded of you. And the things you have prepared, whose will they be?'"

1. God finally says to the rich man, "You fool! This very night your life is being demanded [or "required"] of you." The term "demanded" or "required" is one used in Greek for the repayment of a loan. The rich man's soul is on loan from God and now God wants the loan returned! His goods are a loan. So, too, is his life! And so, tragically, though "his" body is carried out for burial, "his" goods remain behind.

2. Possibly the rich man died soon after building his "maximum security bins." But his security bins gave him no security.

3. Now God asks him, "And the things you have prepared, whose will they be?" The rich man lived alone, planned alone, built alone, indulged alone, and possibly died alone. There was no one to whom he might leave his wealth. He does not even know who will win the power struggle to control his carefully secured wealth after he dies.

4. We are not told the man's response. The parable is open ended. Where did his next dialogue with himself take place, and what did he say?

5. The rich man's silence demands that each of us grapples with the issues the parable raises, and answers God's question in 12:20.

Conclusion

1. The parable concludes with a second wisdom statement, "So it is with those who store up treasures for themselves but are not rich toward God," 12:21. God's endowments are to be used to glorify God through serving others. Those who direct their energy toward enriching themselves are misdirected. Such energy destroys the people that exert it. They fail to understand that humanity is to spend life enriching God!

2. We are not told anything about the response of the initial petitioner. However, he is to learn that the problem is not the division of the inheritance, but a will to serve self rather than to serve God by serving others—including the brother. Jesus challenges the petitioner to look beyond an immediate solution to the need to develop a new perspective.

Jesus and Sirach

1. Sirach 11:18,19 throws light on the message of the parable:

    > One becomes rich through diligence and self-denial,
    >   and the reward allotted to him is this:
    > When he says, "I have found rest,
    >   and now I shall feast on my goods!"
    > he does not know how long it will be
    >   until he leaves them to others and dies.

2. Jesus expands Sirach into a drama with two speakers, with God having the last word. Sirach states that people get wealth by sharp minds and greedy hands. Jesus states that possessions must not be viewed as the end result of human effort, but as the endowment of a gracious God.

3. Sirach encourages people to ask, "What do I do with what I have earned?" Jesus teaches them to ask, "What do I do with what God has made available to me?" Furthermore, Jesus says that not only are "possessions" to be viewed as things God entrusts to people—so also is the soul!

4. Furthermore, while Sirach exposes the lifestyle of those who get rich by sharpness and grabbing, Jesus points to the isolation that the rich man brings into his life. He falls victim to himself. Sirach tells how a man gets his wealth. In Jesus' parable, the man is rich at the outset—and Jesus focuses on how he uses the surpluses.

Though we need some goods for a physical life, more goods do not mean more life! With this thought in mind, the parable presents two warnings: *First*, the desire for material things proves insatiable. *Second*, the abundant life can never be achieved through the accumulation of surpluses.

In "Issues Facing Christianity Today" (1984, p. 213), John Stott writes:

> There are approximately 4.3 billion inhabitants on planet Earth, one-fifth of whom are destitute. The World Business 1978 report, while conceding that there had been for 20 years "unprecedented change and progress in the developing world," went on: "Yet despite this impressive record, some 800 million individuals continue to be trapped in absolute poverty; a condition so characterized by malnutrition, illiteracy, disease, squalid surroundings, high infant mortality and low life expectancy as to be beneath any reasonable definition of human decency." One way to bring this home to us is to consider the provision of clean, safe water. In the West it is piped into our homes and instantly available to us at the turn of a tap. None of us would dream of regarding it as a luxury. We take it for granted. Yet 50% of the Third World population lack it, and 75% of them have no sanitary facilities, so that water-borne diseases kill an estimated 30,000 people every day and fill half the hospital beds of the world.
>
> Meanwhile, whereas one-fifth of the world's population lack the basic necessities for survival, rather more than another one-fifth live in affluence and consume about four-fifths of the world's income. These wealthy nations contribute to the Third World development the derisory sum of $20 billion, while spending 21 times that amount on armaments.

Though the world's population has increased dramatically since Stott wrote, the spirit of the statistics he quotes, and the challenge they present, have changed little. God's people must constantly bear in mind that their goal in life is not to live comfortably, but usefully. They strive to live simply, that others might simply live.

The Great Banquet

Luke 14:15–24

Introduction

1. The parable is introduced by a pious outburst, verse 15: "Blessed is anyone who *eats a meal* in the Kingdom of God." The speaker is pointing forward to the expected Messianic Banquet at the end of the age; see Psalm 23:5; Isaiah 25:6–8.

2. Isaiah 25:6–8 speaks of the coming salvation as a great banquet to which all peoples and nations are invited. (The word "all" occurs five times in these verses.) Gentiles will participate after God has swallowed death and their veil. The *people* swallow the *banquet; God* swallows up *death and the covering.* The veil is *destroyed,* not merely *removed.* Though the nations usually bring gifts to God (Isaiah 18:7, 60:4–7; Psalm 96:8), in Isaiah God sets the banquet before people in pure grace. It is God's gift! The people eat rich food, the food of kings.

3. In the intertestamental period, the notion that Gentiles would participate in the Messianic Age became muted. The vision was lost! The Aramaic Targum translates Isaiah 25:6 as follows:

   > Yahweh of hosts will make for all people in this mountain a meal; and though
   > they suppose it is an honor, it will be a shame for them, and great plagues,
   > plagues from which they will be unable to escape, plagues whereby they will
   > come to their end.

4. 1 Enoch 62:1–16 states that the "kings and the mighty and the exalted and those who rule the earth [the Gentiles] will fall down before the Son of man, who will drive them out of his presence." He will "deliver them to the angels for punishment," (verse 11); "they shall be a spectacle for the righteous" (verse 12); and "his sword is drunk with their blood" (verse 12). After this destruction of sinners, the righteous and elect will eat with the Son of man forever, verse 14.

5. In the Essene community at Qumran, the great banquet was specifically connected with the coming of the Messiah. This is described in a short work called "The Messianic Rule" (1QSa 2:11–22), which states that, in the last days, the Messiah will gather with the whole congregation to eat bread and drink wine. The wise, the intelligent and the perfect will gather with him. These will be assembled by rank. Chapter 2:11 reads:

   > And then [the Messiah] of Israel shall [come]
   > and the chiefs of the [clans of Israel] shall sit before him,
   > [each] in the order of his dignity
   > according to [his place] in their camps and marches.

6. The specifics of rank are carefully spelled out. *First*, the judges and officers. *Second*, the chiefs of thousands, fifties and tens. *Finally*, the Levites. No one is allowed in who is "smitten in his flesh, or paralyzed in his feet or hands, or lame, or blind, or deaf, or smitten in his flesh with a visible blemish." All Gentiles are obviously excluded, and along with them, all imperfect Jews. Thus, Isaiah's vision was blurred, if not eliminated.

7. According to *Isaiah*, the veil of the Gentiles would be destroyed, and they would sit down with God's people. According to *Enoch*, the Gentiles would be excluded. According to the *Qumran community*, all unrighteous Jews and any with a physical blemish would be excluded. The pious guest in Luke 14:15 assumes this background, and invokes a blessing on those who will be accepted on that great day. The expected response from fellow guests would be something like: "O Lord, may we be among the righteous and be counted without blemish, worthy to sit with the men of renown on that great day." However, Jesus does not respond with a traditional pious invocation; He responds with a parable.

The Parable

Frame 1, Luke 14:16: *Then Jesus said to him, "Someone gave a great dinner and invited many.*

---

1. The host is a great man in the community. The guests are his peers and associates.

2. Two invitations are issued. (A double invitation is still the custom in conservative areas of the Middle East.) Because the host must provide meat, he must know how many will attend the banquet so that he can determine what bird or animal will supply the need: chicken, duck, kid, sheep or calf. Once the countdown starts, it cannot be stopped. The animal is killed and must be eaten that night.

3. So, the first invitations are sent out, and acceptances are received. It is a serious invitation, and acceptance of it constitutes a firm commitment. The guest who accepts *must* appear.

Frame 2, Luke 14:17: *At the time for the dinner he sent his slave to say to those who had been invited, 'Come; for everything is now ready.'*

---

1. The host completes preparations. At the appropriate hour, he sends his servant to inform the invited guests that all is ready. See Esther 6:14.

2. In biblical times, when people participated in a banquet, they reclined on couches. Food was placed in front of them, either on the floor or on low tables in large wooden bowls. A wealthy man who gave a great banquet would most likely have had a low table. (Note that the NRSV translates 14:8 and 14:10 incorrectly with "sit.")

The Real Estate Expert

Frame 3, Luke 14:18: *But they all alike began to make excuses. The first said to him, 'I have bought a piece of land, and I must go out and see it; please accept my regrets.'*

---

1. The original Greek translated above as "all alike" might be understood to mean "all at once," or "all" meaning "everyone."

2. The response involves surprise and insult. A last-minute refusal demonstrates the worst of taste and is an affront to the host. The generosity of the host is greeted with an excuse!

3. In the Middle East, no one buys a field without knowing it like the palm of his hand. (Many plots even have proper names.) Before a prospective buyer even *begins* to bargain, he makes himself thoroughly familiar not only with the field, but also with any springs, wells, walls, trees and paths on or near it. He also checks out the average rainfall for the region. All such relevant details are included in any contract that is drawn up.

4. Even more, the purchaser will know the "human history" of the field, namely, who has owned it for generations. He will know the profits it has yielded. Yet the host is expected to believe the man has bought the field unseen!

5. Today the counterpart might be: You refuse a dinner invitation because you have just bought a house and you must now go and examine it and the neighborhood in which it is located!

6. What is the point of looking at a field (or a house!) *after* the purchase procedure? The guest in the parable is saying the purchase is more important than the relationship with the host!

The Plowing Expert

Frame 4, Luke 14:19: Another said, 'I have bought five yoke of oxen, and I am going to try them out; please accept my regrets.'

1. In the Middle East, prospective purchasers of an animal have two procedures open to them.

   a. They can go to a market place, knowing that next to it will be a field where they can test the animal. If the goal is to purchase a team of two animals, they must ensure that the pair can work compatibly.

   b. They can respond to the invitation of an owner who announces, "I have the following animals for sale. Come and watch them at work in my field." After the announcement is made, word about it gets around.

2. The person in the parable has bought not one pair of oxen, but five! That he should have bought them without examining and trying them is ludicrous to the extreme. A modern counterpart would be: A man calls his wife, and says, "I will not be home for dinner tonight. I have just bought five used cars by phone, and must go to the used car lot to check their age and model, and see if they will start!"

3. There is yet another factor. Though animals were considered unclean, the "guest" views the oxen he has purchased as more important than the host.

The Passionate Bridegroom

Frame 5, Luke 14:20: Another said, 'I have just been married, and therefore I cannot come.'

1. The first guest had not yet begun to go to see his field. The second one is on his way to see his oxen. The third guest is going nowhere. He does not talk about what he plans to do, but indicates that he prefers to stay home with his new bride.

2. The man's excuse limps. Even if he had been recently married, the event would not have taken place on the same day as the scheduled banquet. No Middle Eastern village could handle two big events on the same day. They would involve too much competition!

3. An important cultural fact is that men in Middle Eastern society practice restraint in talking about "their women," and in relating to them. To illustrate: A man away from home with two daughters, if writing, will address it to his hoped-for son, not yet born! When Sirach praises the "greats" in the history of Israel, those whom he praises are all men, Sirach chs. 44–50.

4. Furthermore, big meals are held in the middle of the afternoon. The man's excuse is totally inappropriate and out of order. It amounts to: "Yesterday I said I would come. Today I am busy with my new wife—therefore I cannot come." He expects the host to believe that a woman is more important than his banquet. Though such an excuse would be rude in any society, it is intensely rude in the Middle East. Not only that, but the man does not even ask to be excused. His response is guaranteed to infuriate any Middle Eastern host!

The Invitation to Outcasts

Frame 6, Luke 14:21b: Then the owner of the house became angry and said to his slave, 'Go out at once into the streets and lanes of the town and bring in the poor, the crippled, the blind, and the lame.'

1. Though the host is angry with those first invited, he acts in grace to resolve the situation.

2. Apparently, the original guests think their rejection will mean humiliation of the host. It could not proceed without them—the "worthy guests"! These so-called elite are in for a stunning surprise, for the host responds to their refusals by inviting "unworthy guests." He invites those the worthy guests would have considered "riffraff"— those to whom he is not indebted, and those who cannot respond in kind.

3. He sends messages to the poor, maimed, blind and lame from the town. Though those invited are part of the city, they are ostracized from it. They reflect the outcasts whom Jesus sought, and the outcasts who came to Jesus.

Frame 7, Luke 14:21: The blind

Because the blind cannot see, they cannot examine fields—and they will not make the kind of excuse that the "real-estate expert" made.

Frame 8, Luke 14:21: The crippled and the lame

Because the lame experience difficulty in walking, they do not test oxen! Here we have a second radical reversal.

© H.N. Wendt

The poor do not get invited to banquets. They cannot reciprocate!

Frame 10, Luke 14:22,23: And the slave said, 'Sir, what you have ordered has been done, and there is still room.' Then the master said to the slave, 'Go out into the roads and lanes, and compel people to come in, so that my house may be filled. For I tell you, none of those who were invited will taste my dinner.'"

1. Though the servant complies with his master's request in relation to the poor, crippled, blind and lame from the local community, there is still room!

2. The master now sends his servant out among the highways and hedges with the instruction to compel those he finds there to come to his banquet. The "roads" are big roads between bigger towns. The "lanes" are the little paths where most ordinary local people travel; they are often lined with hedges and stone walls.

3. The word "compel" is significant. Those the worthy guests viewed as riffraff would find it hard to believe the host is serious. In the Middle East, the unexpected invitation must be refused—all the more so if those invited are from a lower rank, even if they are half-starving!

4. In the parable, the "unworthy guests" must refuse for about the first fifteen minutes as a matter of honor. They respond, with words or in their minds, with: "How can this be true? Why should your master invite me? What have I ever done for him? I cannot pay him back. The master cannot be serious! He cannot mean it!" So, perhaps the servant grabs them with a smile to convince them that his master is serious, and compels them to accompany him.

    What transpired after the resurrection between Jesus and the two disciples at Emmaus reflects events in the parable, Luke 24:28,29. Though Jesus acted as though he would go further, the two disciples "urged him strongly" to come in!

Frame 10, Luke 14:23: That my house may be filled!

It is possible for the original house to be full without the original guests. The occasion can be a success even with their absence. It must be full—lest the new ones look around and are disappointed that so few came, and conclude that the important people reject him!

The Conclusion

14:24: For I tell you, that none of those who were invited will taste my dinner.

1. Is it the host of the parable speaking to his servant? Or is Jesus talking about His experience? In view of the fact that, in the original Greek, the "you" is plural, Jesus is speaking to the crowd. The meal referred to is His banquet, and He is the host! The banquet is the Messianic Banquet that ushers in the new age. The original guests are the Jewish leaders. The lame and poor of the city are the outcasts within the house of Israel. The guests from the highways and hedges are the Gentiles.

2. Jesus' message to His hearers, the Jewish leaders, is: "The Kingdom has come. The Messianic Age has broken in. All is now ready!" The response He receives consists largely of excuses. After all, He welcomes and eats with sinners! He does not keep the Sabbath in strict fashion. He does not fulfil His hearers' theological and political expectations in relation to the Messianic Age. The guests reclining with Jesus are in danger of excluding themselves from Jesus' great banquet!

3. All through the parable, the servant speaks *as the master*, and people respond to him *as to the master himself.* Similarly, in dealing with Jesus, we deal with God. Jesus' Messianic Banquet is ready for us. It will not be canceled if we do not come; we will just miss out. Others will take our place. We cannot have it delivered by courier while we busy ourselves with other things! If we wish to enjoy it, we must respond and come in.

Walter Trobisch, a pastor and marriage counselor, wrote a small book called "I Loved a Girl." It has been translated into many languages, including over 30 African dialects, and has sold hundreds of thousands of copies. The book sets forth the correspondence between Trobisch and a young man involved in a questionable premarital relationship. The young man's early letters to Trobisch reveal a desire to rationalize and justify his actions. However, his later letters are a cry for help. In one of his letters, Trobisch tells the young man that, above all else, he must "restore his lines of communication with God."

Some years ago while addressing a group of clergy in Adelaide, South Australia, Trobisch reported that he had received proximately 12,000 letters from people all around the world about the book. Significantly, almost every one of those letters was a plea for help from someone wanting to know how to restore his or her lines of communication with God.

Pleas sometimes came in more direct ways. On one occasion, a young Japanese woman who had been studying in the United States came to the Trobisch's home in Austria. She was on her way back to Japan and carried with her a Japanese translation she had made of "I Loved a Girl." She said that she had read the book while in the United States, and was sure that it could help many young people in Japan—hence, her translation efforts. However, she said there were some words, phrases and concepts she wanted Trobisch to clarify for her. What, for example, did he mean by "restoring the lines of communication with God"?

She regretted that she had only one day available, but Trobisch assured her that was enough time for the project. They set to work! Eventually she said that she saw the implications of what he was saying and would now be able to express what he had written in her own language more clearly. When their discussion time came to an end, she said that she would like to express her joy at the new insights through traditional dance forms; she was, after all, a trained Japanese dancer. The Trobisch family was enthralled by her performance in their home that evening.

Next morning, Trobisch took her back to the railroad station. She boarded her train, and kept talking to him through the window until departure time. As the train pulled away from Trobisch, she looked back at him and literally shouted, "I did not come for help with translation at all! I came for help to restore my own lines of communication with God!" She had gone to all the trouble of translating Trobisch's book into Japanese just to have an excuse to meet with him to discuss the problems that had been plaguing her own conscience.

The parable of the Great Banquet describes people devising ways to reject God's invitation into His Kingdom. The story of the would-be translator describes a person doing everything possible to discover on what terms one might be invited to participate in the Messianic Banquet.

The Lost Sheep
and
The Lost Coin

Luke 15:1–10

Introduction

1. Luke 15 contains three of Jesus' best known parables: the Lost Sheep, the Lost Coin, and the Two Lost Sons. The third of these will be dealt with in the following unit. These three parables do not set out to *present* the Gospel, but to *vindicate* the Gospel. Throughout, Jesus is described as defending his association with sinners. The opening two verses of Luke 15 state:

    > Now all the tax collectors and sinners were coming near to listen to Jesus. And the Pharisees and the scribes were grumbling and saying, "This fellow welcomes sinners and eats with them."

2. Table fellowship anywhere in the world is a relatively serious matter. This was, and still is, especially true in the Middle East. To invite someone to share a meal is to bestow a great honor on that person. To share table is to share life. It is an offer of peace, trust, brotherhood and forgiveness. When Jesus shares meals with publicans and sinners, He expresses the message of His mission in action. He lives out the message of the redeeming love of God.

3. In the Middle East today, as in the past, a nobleman may feed any number of needy persons, lower in rank than himself, as a sign of his generosity, but he does not *eat* with them. However, when guests are "received," the one receiving the guests eats with them. The meal is a special sign of acceptance. The text presents Jesus as engaging in some such social relationship with publicans and sinners.

4. In addition to eating with sinners, it is possible that Jesus was Himself the host at the meal. The accusation, "This fellow welcomes sinners and eats with them," is closely parallel to Mark 2:15–17 where Jesus is clearly the host for the meal. The same may be true in Luke 15:2. The word Luke uses for "welcomes" does often imply hospitality.

5. If this is the intent in Luke 15:2, it is very significant, for, as in any Oriental banquet, it is assumed that the guest brings great honor to the house in which he is being entertained. The host begins by referring to the honor brought to his house by the guests. The guests can then respond by invoking the honor of

Parables Unit 6-1

God on the noble host and by affirming that they, too, have received honor by being in the host's presence.

6. Even if modern village banquet customs are considered too recent to be used as evidence in determining ancient customs, it can certainly be affirmed that for Jesus to host sinners would have been a much more serious offense to the Pharisees than merely to eat with sinners informally or to accept their invitations, e.g. Zacchaeus, Luke 19:1–10. Thus it is little wonder that Jesus' table fellowship with sinners offended the cultural and theological sensitivities of the Pharisees. Little wonder that they grumble, "This fellow welcomes sinners and eats with them," 15:2.

The Lost Sheep
Luke 15:3–7

[3]So Jesus told them this parable: "[4]Which of you, having a hundred sheep and losing one of them, does not leave the ninety-nine in the wilderness and go after the one that is lost until he finds it? [5]When he finds it, he lays it on his shoulders and rejoices. [6]And when he comes home, he calls together his friends and his neighbors, saying to them, 'Rejoice with me, for I have found my sheep that was lost.' [7]Just so, I tell you, there will be more joy in heaven over one sinner who repents than over ninety-nine righteous persons who need no repentance."

1. The parables of the Lost Sheep and the Lost Coin (15:8–10) may be viewed as a double parable, with the second reinforcing the themes of the first.

2. People living in Palestine, Syria and Lebanon tell us that anyone wealthy enough to own a hundred sheep will hire a shepherd, or let some less affluent member of the extended family take care of them.

3. Among the less affluent, the average family may have five to fifteen animals. Common practice is for a number of families to get together and hire a shepherd. The shepherd may himself own some of the animals and be from one of the families.

4. Where a herd consists of about forty animals, the shepherd leading them may be their sole owner. Where a herd consists of a hundred sheep, the shepherd leading them is probably not their sole owner. Thus, "to have a hundred sheep" can mean "to be responsible for a hundred sheep." It need not necessarily mean to own a hundred sheep.

5. It is unlikely that the shepherd in the parable is merely a hireling or a stranger. The sheep he is caring for belong to the extended family. He is a member of that extended family and naturally feels responsible to the entire family clan; any loss is a loss to all of them. This understanding of the culture clarifies the joy in the community reflected at the center of the parable. In short, the extended family loses if a sheep is lost; the whole clan rejoices if the lost is found. The story runs as follows:

Frame 1

To answer His accusers (verse 1,2), Jesus tells them a parable, verse 3. He tells them about a shepherd, who, while caring for a hundred sheep, loses one, verse 4. How, we are not told. A certain negligence on the shepherd's part is implied, though it is not a key factor in determining the parable's meaning.

Frame 2

The sheep strayed without being aware that it was straying. Suddenly, it senses that something is wrong and that it is lost. It does not cry out for the shepherd, or go looking for him. Rather, the shepherd goes looking for the sheep. The sheep is "found." Shepherds in Galilee inform us that a lost sheep will lie down helplessly and refuse to budge.

Frame 3

After the sheep is found, it must be restored. This implies that the shepherd must lift the sheep (of considerable weight), place it around his shoulders, and carry it back to the village—possibly a long distance. Even so, he rejoices twice: first, when he finds it and while he carries it, and second, when he arrives back in the village. The theme of "joy" is prominent throughout.

Frame 4

When the shepherd returns to his village, the community rejoices—for two reasons: *First*, the community rejoices to hear that the shepherd is safe. *Second*, the flock is most likely owned by these same friends and neighbors. The lost sheep is a community loss. The recovered sheep is an occasion for joy for all the neighbors.

Additional Insights

1. The telling of a parable about a shepherd in an address to Pharisees has a special problem. Moses was accepted as a shepherd. A *midrash* on Exodus records a story of Moses searching out a lost kid and being told by God that he will lead Israel. Kings were referred to by Ezekiel as shepherds (Ezekiel 34), and God himself was thought of as a shepherd, Psalm 23. Thus the figure of the shepherd was a noble symbol.

2. However, in Jesus' day, flesh-and-blood shepherds who wandered around after sheep were classified as unclean "people of the land." For the Pharisee, a "sinner" was either an immoral person who did not keep the law or a person engaged in one of the proscribed trades, among which was herding sheep.

3. It is difficult to know how the rabbis managed to revere the shepherd of the Old Testament and despise the shepherd who herded the neighbor's sheep. But this seems to have been the case.

4. The parable, addressed to Pharisees (15:1–3), must have shocked their sensitivities. Any man who believed shepherds were unclean would naturally be offended if addressed as one. Yet Jesus begins, "Which one of you, having a hundred sheep"—words which can be understood as an indirect and yet very powerful attack on the Pharisaic attitudes toward proscribed professions.

   To show deference to the Pharisees' feelings in this matter, Jesus would have had to begin the parable something like this: "Which man of you owning a hundred sheep, if he heard that the hired shepherd had lost one, would he not summon the shepherd and demand that the sheep be found under threat of fine?" It is very doubtful that any Pharisee would have taken up the task of a shepherd under any condition. Thus, the decision to address Pharisees as shepherds is a culturally and theologically conditioned decision of some significance.

5. A further question is raised by the phrase "in the wilderness," 15:4. The shepherd leaves the flock "in the wilderness." He then returns home with the lost sheep on his shoulders. The bedouin shepherd lives in the wilderness and does not return to a village at night. The peasant shepherd does return the sheep to his home in the village each evening, and herds the sheep into the courtyard of the family home at the end of each day. This factor, and the reference to the "home" in verse 6, suggest that Jesus is referring to peasant shepherds in this parable.

6. In Syria, Palestine or Mesopotamia, one does not see a flock attended by a single person. Two (and even three) shepherds are commonly employed. When a sheep is lost and the shepherd goes to seek it, the other shepherd takes the flock home. When the second shepherd arrives at the village, the neighbors would at once notice the absence of the first shepherd or they would be told of it, for though they would be concerned about the loss of the animal, they would be more concerned about the safety of the man. Should he encounter a wild beast, the lone shepherd, with only his stick and sling, is in a perilous predicament. The finding and bringing home of the lost sheep is, therefore, a matter of great thanksgiving in the community. Still today, village men gather almost nightly to discuss the events of the village, recite poetry, and tell stories from the oral tradition.

7. The text, then, can mean "he left the flock while they were still in the wilderness." The point is that the shepherd counted the flock while they were still in the wilderness, not after they got back to the village. After discovering that one was missing, he naturally departed from them "in the wilderness," leaving a second shepherd to guide the flock back to the village. Thus the leaving of the sheep in the wilderness need not be viewed as an unauthentic element in the story. At the same time it must be observed that the ninety-nine are left hanging. We know the lost sheep got home; we are not told what happened to the ninety-nine.

8. The final words of verse 4 state, "until he finds it." The shepherd of Palestine has indeed to search "until he finds it" in the sense that he either has to bring back a live animal or its remains, as proof that he has not sold it.

The Themes

1. The parable contains at least four important themes that must be seen in relationship to each other. These are:

    a. *The joy of the shepherd:* His joy is one that is expressed in, and shared with, a community. This theme, which occurs also in the parable of the Lost Coin, points to God's joy over the conversion of sinners.

    b. *The burden of restoration:* The wandering sheep must be brought back to the fold now gathered in the village. This, for any shepherd, has a price, as does also the act of restoration. In telling the parable, Jesus defends His welcome of sinners—a welcome that involves restoration to a community. For Jesus, the burden of restoration points in the direction of the passion.

    c. *The gracious love that seeks the sinner:* People go to endless trouble to recover lost property, and experience deep satisfaction when they succeed. Even the publicans and sinners belong to God— despite all appearances to the contrary. God wants them back and goes to great lengths to win them back to Himself.

d. *Repentance:* The parable raises two questions in relationship to repentance. The first is, "Who is expected to repent?" The second is, "What is the nature of this repentance?"

The background to the first question is found in the rabbinic debate over the so-called "completely righteous." Some rabbis affirmed that there were indeed "completely righteous" persons whom God loved in a special way. Another opinion affirmed that God's greatest love was extended to repentant sinners. This debate is reflected in the Talmud, which reads:

> R. Hiyya b. Abba also said in R. Johanan's name, "All the prophets prophesied only for repentant sinners; but as for the perfectly righteous (who had never sinned at all), 'the eye hath not seen, O God, beside thee, what he hath prepared for him that waiteth for him.'"

2. In this text Rabbi Abba is affirming that there are "the perfectly righteous." God loves them more than He does repentant sinners. The Talmud then offers the opinion of Rabbi Abbahu, who thinks "repentant sinners" are closer to God than these "perfectly righteous." He is in turn answered by an affirmation of the first opinion, namely, that God prefers the "completely righteous."

3. However, some centuries earlier, Sirach wrote, "Do not revile a repentant sinner; remember that we all are guilty," 11:53. This text seems to deny the category of the "perfectly righteous." Such a denial is in keeping with Isaiah 53:6, where all sheep are reported to have gone astray.

4. Jesus' view is more in harmony with Isaiah and Sirach than with the Talmud. In the first three Gospels, the theme of "the perfectly righteous" is not apparent, but the universal need for all to repent is affirmed. Thus, in line with Sirach and Isaiah 53:6, the reference in Luke 15:7 to "the ninety-nine righteous persons who need no repentance" is perhaps best understood as irony. For Jesus, all are lost sheep who need a shepherd to guide them. All people must repent.

5. But to revert once again to the "ninety-nine left in the wilderness": The listener does not know if they are home or not. Jesus *may* be saying, with some irony, "The angels cannot rejoice over the ninety-nine 'righteous' because they are not yet home."

6. This brings us to the question of the nature and function of this repentance. For first-century Judaism, repentance was a way of *bringing in* the kingdom. In the preaching of Jesus, repentance was a *response* to the kingdom *already come*. For the rabbis, repentance was a precondition for grace; it was a work by which a righteous man showed himself righteous.

7. All this is clearly silenced in the parable of the Lost Sheep. The sheep does nothing to prompt the shepherd to begin his search except to become lost. In the parable, the shepherd finds the sheep. Then, in the conclusion to the parable, there is reported "joy over one sinner who repents." Here "being found" is equated with "repentance." Thus the parable of the Lost Sheep sets out a radically new understanding of the nature of repentance.

Summary

Four theological themes interlock in the parable: joy in restoration to community; joy in the burden of that restoration; unconditional grace that seeks the lost; and a new understanding of repentance.

The Lost Coin

Luke 15:8–10

---

⁸Or what woman having ten silver coins, if she loses one of them, does not light a lamp, sweep the house, and search carefully until she finds it? ⁹When she has found it, she calls together her friends and neighbors, saying, "Rejoice with me, for I have found the coin that I had lost." ¹⁰Just so, I tell you, there is joy in the presence of the angels of God over one sinner who repents.

© H.N. Wendt

The message of the illustrations is as follows:

Frame 1

A woman counts the coins she has in her possession, only to find that one is missing. She is deeply concerned.

Frame 2

She lights a lamp, gets her broom, and sweeps the house.

Frame 3

She persists in her search until she finds the missing coin.

Frame 4

After finding the coin, she calls her friends and neighbors together and invites them to rejoice with her.

Though there is reference to a "double joy" in the parable of the Lost Sheep, the theme of joy is not doubled in this parable. The reason for this is obvious. In the case of the parable of the Lost Coin, there is no burden of restoration. Once the coin is found, it is automatically restored. Yet the theme of joy does appear in the center and at the end, and is therefore the parable's high point. Though the theme of "the burden of restoration" is missing, the themes of grace, repentance and joy are stressed.

Cultural Elements

Several cultural elements need to be noted.

1. The introduction is shortened to "which woman," because to have said "which woman of you" to a group of Oriental men would have been an unpardonable insult.

2. The coin in question is a *drachma*, and represented about a day's wage.

3. To a large extent, a peasant village is self-supporting, making its own cloth and growing its own food. Cash is a rare commodity. The loss of a coin is a sad event. Hence the lost coin is of far greater value in a peasant home than the day's labor it represents monetarily.

4. It has often been observed that the coin may be a part of the woman's jewelry or dowry. However, a distinction must be made between the bedouin and the villager. Bedouin women wear their dowry in the form of coins hanging on their veils; village women do not.

5. The movement of peasant women in the village was and is extremely limited. This woman clearly knew that the coin was in the house. She had not been out. Her diligence was prompted by the knowledge that she would find the coin if she persisted in her sweeping.

6. In the cultural world of first-century Palestine, the very use of a woman in an illustration required a moral decision. Jesus is again rejecting Pharisaic attitudes toward groups of people in society. First it was the proscribed shepherds, now the "inferior" woman.

7. Two aspects of the imagery in the parable of the Lost Sheep are intensified in the parable of the Lost Coin. *First*, the relative value of the thing lost is intensified. It is now one in ten, not one in a hundred—and, as we have noted, the coin may have had a value beyond its monetary worth. *Second*, the place of search for the lost is more narrowly confined. It is now the confines of a house, not the wide wilderness. Thus the assurance is intensified that the lost one can be found if the searcher is willing to expend sufficient effort.

The story that follows reflects some of the spirit of the parables of the Lost Sheep and the Lost Coin (and the Two Lost Sons, Unit 7):

A man riding on a train noticed a young man across the aisle who was highly agitated. He kept looking at his watch, then glancing out the window, and was unable to sit still for more than a few seconds at a time. The man asked the youth what the problem was, and was told the following story:

Several years earlier the young man had run away from home simply because his parents had not given him his own way in some matter of minor importance. Though he knew it would break their hearts, he had stubbornly persisted in not writing to them, so that for several years they had no knowledge of his whereabouts or his activities. Finally, filled with remorse as well as homesickness, he had written to his parents to say that he would like to come back home—if they were willing to have him. To know whether or not they would forgive him and welcome him back to their home, he suggested that they tie a cloth to a pear tree in the corner of their orchard, which he could see from the train window as he went past their farm just before arriving at their railroad station. The cloth would indicate their willingness to forgive and receive him, and he would then get off the train. If no cloth appeared, he would know that he was not welcome and would continue on the train.

He confided to the older man that soon they would be passing the family farm and he was filled with agony and suspense wondering what the answer would be. The older man said that he would look, and if the answer was negative he would try to soften the announcement. The younger man agreed, described the characteristics that would make the farm recognizable, and told the man they would pass it in about one minute. The older man looked out the window as the train rolled past the family farm; then—smiling—turned to the young man and said, "It is all right, son, you are forgiven. There is a cloth tied to every tree in the orchard!"

The Two Lost Sons

Luke 15:11–32

Introduction

1. A Pharisaic commentary on the Law said: "There is joy before God when those who provoke Him perish from the world." In Luke 15:7, Jesus says: "There will be more joy in heaven over one sinner who repents than over ninety-nine righteous persons who need no repentance."

2. The parable under review is perhaps Jesus' best-known parable. It has been variously called the parable of the prodigal son, and the parable of the waiting father. In this study, it will be referred to as the parable of the two lost sons, for the very good reason that it tells of a son who was lost *at a distance* and of a son who was lost though he stayed *at home*.

3. Jesus had stirred up a hornet's nest in Galilee, and He is now on His way to Jerusalem, Luke 9:51. Though the tax collectors and sinners gather around Jesus to hear what He has to say to them, the scribes and Pharisees murmur saying, "This fellow welcomes sinners and eats with them." Jesus knows full well that, when He finally enters Jerusalem, opposition to him will explode.

4. *Tax collectors:* It is difficult for us in the Western world to understand the level of hatred ordinary people felt toward those who collaborated with an occupying power to collect taxes for them. A "tax farmer" bought, from the ruling power, the right to collect taxes in a certain area. He then hired local people to do the actual collecting. Graft and corruption were the order of the day.

5. *Sinners:* The scribes and Pharisees lumped together sinners, adulterers, the unclean and the breakers of the law, and rejected them as being beyond redemption. Luke tells us that Jesus "received" these sinners. The word he uses states that Jesus accepted them as His brothers and sisters. More, Jesus ate with them. In the Middle East, friendship is one thing. But to eat with a person is virtually a sacramental act in which participants declare total acceptance of each other.

6. When Luke says that the scribes and Pharisees were "grumbling" because Jesus was welcoming tax collectors and sinners into full fellowship with Himself, the word Luke uses for "grumbling" is the word the Greek Old Testament uses for the Israelites' repeated murmurings against Moses in the wilderness. Note also that when Jesus told the scribes and Pharisees the parables of the lost sheep, the lost coin, and the lost sons, He was speaking to a very specific group of people.

7. Luke does not tell us what the older son finally did to his father. This points to the challenge that Jesus was presenting to the scribes and Pharisees. He was saying, "Yes, I do welcome sinners and eat with them. That is at the heart of My ministry. That is what the kingdom of God is all about. What will

you do about it? What will you do with Me?" Their murmurings would eventually give rise to "Crucify Him!"

The Parable

Frame 1, Luke 15:11–13a: *[11]Then Jesus said, "There was a man who had two sons. [12]The younger of them said to his father, 'Father, give me the share of the property that will belong to me.' So he divided his property between them. [13a]A few days later the younger son gathered all he had and traveled to a distant country...*

---

1. There are those who, in this parable, see two stories. The first is about a son who runs away, and the second is about a son who stays at home—but not so! Jesus begins, "There was a man who had two sons." The parable is about *three* people: *a man and his two sons.* In many ways, the older son is the key figure.

2. First, the younger son says: "Father, give me the share of property that will belong to me." The request can mean only one thing. The younger son is impatient for his father's death. Traditionally, a father's wealth would be divided only *after* his death. On very rare occasions, a father *could*, on his own initiative, divide the property while he was still living. Though he assigned his property over to a son, the father still retained control over it. In short, a son was given the right of *possession* but not the right of *disposition.* However, what the younger son demands is not merely *the right of possession* but also *the right of disposition.*

3. When people in the Middle East hear this parable today, from Algeria to Iran, from the Sudan to Syria, the response is the same: "Impossible! This father should beat his son! His son wants him to die!" Even so, the father divides the property. He assigns two-thirds to the older son, and one-third to the younger son. Note that the younger son does not break a specific law in requesting the division. Deuteronomy 21:17 states that a younger son should receive a third. However, he breaks his father's heart, for he wants his share *now*—and *in cash*!

4. This raises another point. The son's request hurts not only his father, but the entire family clan. The wealth of a village family is not held in a savings account. It is held in the family's house and buildings, and in animals and land. In our story, the land and animals would have had to be sold quickly at any price. In the Middle East, people can haggle for days over the smallest transaction. Those who sell in a hurry sell cheaply. For a family to lose one-third of its assets would be a staggering loss.

5. Note also that the son does not state: "I want my *inheritance.*" He states: "Give me the share of the property that will belong to me." He avoids using the word *inheritance.* To accept one's *inheritance* is to accept a leadership responsibility in the clan. The recipient is duty bound to administer the property on behalf of the family, to settle quarrels, to defend the honor of the family against all comers (even with his life), to increase the family's wealth, to represent the family nobly at village weddings, feasts and funerals. However, this boy wants no *responsibility.* He wants only the *money.*

6. Through his actions, the younger son cuts himself off from his roots. In cutting himself off from his father, he cuts himself off from his *real* inheritance. A man's security in a village is his family. His family is his insurance, his old-age pension, his assurance of marriage, and his physical and emotional well-being. These things are as precious as life itself. Still today in the Middle East, when you ask a person where he is from, he does not give you his address. He replies: "I am from such and such a village." He may never have been there, but his roots are there. If he is out of work or in need of

friends, he will be welcomed, even if the villagers have never seen him. All will open their doors to him, and will accept him totally. So, when the younger son makes his request, he substitutes the *passing* for the *permanent*. In so doing, he breaks his father's heart and all relationships with his family.

7. The older son certainly knows the entire story. In a Middle Eastern village community, everything that happens is known almost immediately by everyone. Perhaps the conversation between the father and the younger son is overheard by the servants or other members of the family. Perhaps the older son is present. Whatever the case might have been, the older son refuses to honor his obligations and duty.

8. In a village quarrel, people involved in a dispute never make up directly. To do so is to require someone to lose face. The reconciliation takes place through a third party. The "go-between" moves back and forth between the disputing parties until a solution is reached that both can accept. The mediator then arranges a meeting in which those involved in a conflict meet, shake hands, embrace, and perhaps kiss each other. The mediator is always chosen on the basis of the strength of his relationship with the quarreling parties. In our story, the older son would have been the natural choice for mediator. And he must begin immediately. He must do so, even if he hates his brother. He must act for the sake of his father. He must say things such as: "O my brother, your father is an old man. You may not see him again—do not leave us! O my brother, your mother will go blind weeping. We cannot bear the thought of you leaving us!" But he does not do so. Apparently things are bad between him and his brother, and between him and his father. And so, the father grants his younger son permission to turn away from him. However, he does not sever his relationship with the son. Had he disowned him, there would have been no possibility of reconciliation. Because he does not disown him, the possibility of reconciliation remains.

9. Perhaps during the days immediately prior to his departure, the younger son exchanges his inheritance for a sack of coins. After all, he must be able to carry his inheritance with him. As he leaves, the scorn of the village is considerable. The only thing that goes with him is the love of a brokenhearted father. It is significant to note that the word Luke uses to describe his departure is: "He traveled away from his own people." He leaves—and loses—his village!

Frame 2, Luke 15:13b–16: *¹³ᵇ...and there squandered his property in dissolute living. ¹⁴When he had spent everything, a severe famine took place throughout that country, and he began to be in need. ¹⁵So he went and hired himself out to one of the citizens of that country, who sent him to his fields to feed the pigs. ¹⁶He would gladly have filled himself with the pods that the pigs were eating; and no one gave him anything.*

---

1. In the unnamed "far country" to which the son goes, he squanders his property. We are not told how. The tradition that he spent it on immoral living is based on the older brother's later slanderous remarks, 15:30. We must bear in mind that, in leaving the village, the younger son cut himself off from his original community. He now needs a new circle of friends—a new family. Hence, it is possible that he spends the money foolishly to establish a reputation for generosity among his new associates. Perhaps he throws lavish parties. Perhaps he tries to buy new friendships by giving expensive gifts. Naturally, while he has money, he has friends. When he has no money, he has no friends. He is now in real trouble. What is he to do?

2. First, he tries to get a job. Jesus says he literally "glued" himself to a local "citizen" in the hope that the man might employ him. If the man is a citizen, he is a man of some standing in the community. Most likely he knows the would-be employee is a Jew and that he once had access to money. He also possibly hopes that by offering him a job feeding pigs, the Jewish job-seeker will turn the offer down and leave him alone.

3. The situation is complicated by the fact that, in the world of Jesus' day, pigs were not housed in pens or sties. They wandered along public roads and paths. They served as the community's garbage disposal units. Therefore, in caring for them, the son would be very much on public display. Surely he would never accept such a position!

4. But, because he is desperate, he does. That makes him a slave, an outcast, in Jewish eyes. And while he cares for the pigs, he holds out his hands to passersby in the hope that they will give him something. (If you have ever wandered around the streets of Bombay or similar cities, you will know how emotionally unnerving it is for both beggar and begged-of when their eyes meet!) But no one gives him anything. What is he to do? He needs money to buy food to stay alive. At stake is his very survival.

Frame 3, Luke 15:17–20a: *[17]But when he came to himself he said, 'How many of my father's hired hands have bread enough and to spare, but here I am dying of hunger! [18]I will get up and go to my father, and I will say to him, "Father, I have sinned against heaven and before you; [19]I am no longer worthy to be called your son; treat me like one of your hired hands."' [20a]So he set off and went to his father.*

---

1. There is only one course open to him: He must return home. And he must do so while he still has enough strength to walk the distance. But he has to devise a strategy—for three reasons. *First*, remembering that his father did not subject him to harsh discipline when he made his initial request, he most likely suspects that his father will not reject him. *Second*, he must face his brother's scorn and "eat his brother's bread," and so be indebted to his brother as well as his father. If his brother has treated him badly before, he will treat him worse now! *Third*, he must face the village community. He has broken all relationships with them, and is despised by them. When he gets to the edge of the village, he simply cannot march through it to his father's house and say, "Here I am, father!" He must stop at the edge of the village, send a message to his father, and wait for hours and even days to see if his father will respond and agree to meet with him. And village society is ruthless when a man is down!

2. He works out a plan. He will return to his father and tell him that, though he has sinned against God and his father and is no longer worthy to be called his father's son, he asks only that his father will help him by letting him become an apprentice and learn a trade. And here he reveals his strategy for survival. By working at a trade, he can support himself, possibly even pay back some of the family money that he squandered, and perhaps regain a little dignity in the eyes of his community. And because he will not have to live in or near the family home, but in the village, he will not have to come into constant contact with his brother.

3. The long walk back to his father, brother and village begins. But note! He has not yet repented! The issue at stake is his *physical survival*!

Frame 4, Luke 15:20b-24: *[20b]But while he was still far off, his father saw him and was filled with compassion; and he ran and put his arms around him and kissed him. [21]Then the son said to him, 'Father, I have sinned against heaven and before you; I am no longer worthy to be called your son.' [22]But the father said to his slaves, 'Quickly, bring out a robe—the best one—and put it on him; put a ring on his finger and sandals on his feet. [23]And get the fatted calf and kill it, and let us eat and celebrate; [24]for this son of mine was dead and is alive again; he was lost and is found!' And they began to celebrate.*

52

1. While all this is going on, what is the father doing? Has he forgotten his son? Impossible! We can well imagine that he thinks about him daily and anxiously. We can well imagine that he thinks about him each night prior to surrendering himself to sleep, and asks: "Where is my boy? Does he have food? Does he have friends? Is he well? Is he alive?" And we might well imagine that, from time to time, he looks down the road on which his son has walked away from him, and asks. "Will my boy ever come back to me?"

2. One day, while looking down that road, he sees someone on the horizon—walking toward the village. He wonders who it might be. If only it were his son! But he must not let his imagination run away with him. Many people have walked along that road. But the more he looks, the more he suspects something. Is it? Could it really be...? Surely not! But finally he knows! *My boy! It is my boy! My boy is coming back to me!"* And he runs to meet his son.

3. We Westerners think little about the fact that he runs. People in many other cultures react differently—they smile! In many parts of the world still today, as in Jesus' day, old men never run. Little boys run. Teenagers run. Old men never run. They walk slowly, with great dignity. But this father runs! He must get to the boy first. Why? The villagers, the villagers! When the son asked his father to give him the share of the property that was due to him, he did not sin merely against his father. He sinned against the village! He has no right to return to it. More, if the villagers see him returning and get to him first, they have every right to beat him or to throw stones at him to drive him away—and even to kill him. So the father must get to his boy first! How the father receives the son will determine how the villagers must receive him.

4. In running, literally "racing" to his son, the father demeans himself. To run, he must hold up his outer garment that he might move swiftly. He exposes his undershirt—if you like, his underwear! And, without doubt, the boys and teenagers of the village run alongside him, laughing loudly, pointing at his exposed legs and knees, and saying, "Look! His legs! His underwear! Ha, ha, ha!" But the father is prepared to demean himself to get to that boy first!

5. Finally, the two meet. An *obedient* son has the right to kiss his father's hands. This *wayward* son has only the right to fall to the ground and kiss his father's feet. But the father will not let him fall to the ground. Though the father says nothing, he takes his son in his arms, holds him up, and kisses him. The boy tries to deliver his little speech—but succeeds in getting out only the first part of it: "Father, I have sinned against God and you, and am no longer worthy to be called your son." But he does not get out the bit about becoming an apprentice and learning a trade. Why?

6. The father takes over and does the talking! "Place the best robe in the house around him. Place a ring on his finger. Put shoes on his feet. Kill the fatted calf and prepare a feast!" Note the incredible implications! The father accepts the boy back as his son, and reinstates him in the household. The best robe?—most likely the best robe from the father's own wardrobe. A ring?—that was a symbol of authority in the household. Shoes?—only slaves go barefoot; sons wear shoes. Son? Yes! Hired servant? Apprentice? Never! He orders the servants to serve his son! Everyone in the village must now treat the son in conformity with the father's wishes. The father's actions have stated the way things are to be.

7. The father calls for a feast! There must be a feast to celebrate! He instructs that the family's fatted calf (an expensive item!) be part of the menu. And do remember that, in a sense, that fatted calf belongs to the older brother!

8. In that part of the world still today, a village feast is a truly special event. In the situation described in the parable, the father is the focus of attention. He has decided the nature of the son's reception, and decreed the future relationship. He sits in the center of the house, and all the guests come in to him and

5

thank him for inviting them. He, in turn, thanks them for honoring him with their presence. On this particular occasion, the guest of honor is the younger son. No person in the village dare say anything unkind to him. They may not like what he has done, and may not feel well disposed toward him. But they must accept and welcome him. The father's actions have determined what theirs must be.

9. But now comes the rub. Who is to be the "head waiter," so to say? The older brother! Though the other servants would do the bulk of the work, the older son must be present to set the tone of the hospitality offered by assuring the guests that they are most welcome, and that they honor the family by coming!

Frame 5, Luke 15:25–32: *²⁵Now his elder son was in the field; and when he came and approached the house, he heard music and dancing. ²⁶He called one of the slaves and asked what was going on. ²⁷He replied, 'Your brother has come, and your father has killed the fatted calf, because he has got him back safe and sound.' ²⁸Then he became angry and refused to go in. His father came out and began to plead with him. ²⁹But he answered his father, 'Listen! For all these years I have been working like a slave for you, and I have never disobeyed your command; yet you have never given me even a young goat so that I might celebrate with my friends. ³⁰But when this son of yours comes back, who has devoured your property with prostitutes, you killed the fatted calf for him!' ³¹Then the father said to him, 'Son, you are always with me, and all that is mine is yours. ³²But we had to celebrate and rejoice, because this brother of yours was dead and has come to life; he was lost and has been found.'"*

---

1. But the older son is not home when the banquet begins. He is out in the fields. No—he is not working. He is the older son in a household of some wealth. The family has a home, servants, fields and cattle. He does not work, but he supervises. Most likely he is lying under the shade of a tree, nibbling away at some fruit, watching over the hired servants, and paying them their wages at the end of the day.

2. When he finally returns to the family home, no doubt there are boys running around outside enjoying themselves. Even though they are not part of the festivities, they know what is going on. Within half an hour of the son's return, everyone in the village knows what is happening. The older son asks one of the boys, "What's going on around here?" The lad replies, "Your brother has come, and your father has killed the fatted calf." (A servant would never have referred to "the master" as "your father.") The older brother is furious. He will not go in. And within a manner of moments, all in the house sense the tension. The atmosphere is electric, to say the least. The eating, music and dancing stop. All eyes turn toward the father.

3. The situation must be resolved. But how? The father should not leave his place of honor. He should stay inside among his guests! To go outside would be again demeaning. Even so, out he goes—to face the older son's fury and insults!

4. The older son explodes with, "Father, you've never done anything like this for me! You have not even given me a kid goat from the flock to share with my friends. And I've worked all these years for you. Yet, when this son of yours [note: *your son*, not *my brother*] comes back, this son who has been wasting his substance on harlots, you kill the fatted calf!" The father replies with great concern and kindness, "My son, [and he uses a very tender word here] all that I have is yours! You see, we thought *your brother* [note that term!] was dead—but he is alive. We thought he was lost—but he has been found!"

5. Let's give some thought to the older son's thinking patterns. He has never left his father. He has stayed home and carried out his duties. His father should be impressed with his track record, and see himself as indebted to his older son. However, he says the father has never shown him any special

favor. He has never even given him so much as a kid goat to share with his friends at a feast! (His "friends" are people "out there," not members of the family or the immediate community.) He feels he has done so much, but received so little. More, as he sees it, the father has demeaned the family reputation by welcoming back this womanizing vagabond!

6. What does he do to his father? We are not told. Possibly, in his rage he beat him—or even killed him. These suggestions are not farfetched if we bear in mind that those to whom Jesus told this parable eventually screamed, "Crucify Him! Crucify Him!"

7. The father in the parable does not impose laws and constraints on his sons. He does not force them to do things against their will. He lets them do their worst to him so that he might do his best for them. And if the older son did indeed opt to beat his father, perhaps the father's hope was that he would eventually come to his senses and ask: "What am I doing? How can I possibly do this to my father? What kind of a father do I have, who lets me do this to him? Why does he act this way toward me?" And if the older son does get around to asking these questions, his whole relationship with his father and brother will change.

8. Let's say that, as the weeks go by and things settle down, the younger boy goes back to work in the family circle. Can you imagine the spirit in which he does that? Can you imagine the difference the villagers see in him? Can you imagine how he relates to the servants in the household? And perhaps some, who do not know the family story, ask him, "Why are you like this—so kind, concerned and compassionate?" To such questions, the younger son might well reply, "Have you never heard my story? Let me tell it to you!"

9. What changed the younger son? When he came to his senses in the far country, he did not repent. He simply realized that he was in a dangerous situation. There was a drought in the land, and a severe shortage of food. His own survival was at stake. His concern was to save his life and regain some of the security that he had enjoyed prior to his departure. The thing that changed him was the look he saw on his father's face and the welcome he received. He was "found."

10 Briefly, what does this parable mean for us? We are the ones who have wandered away from God. We are the ones who have claimed ownership of creation and life, and want to use them to enjoy ourselves, rather than use them to glorify God and serve others in our earthly village. And when we come to our senses and return to our Heavenly Father, what do we have to bring? The younger son had only pig-stink to bring with him. We have only sin-stink to bring with us. But when we come, the heavenly Father rushes out to meet us, welcomes us passionately, and reinstates us in His family circle. God "finds" us.

In many parts of Africa, when a dispute takes place in a village, this is what happens: In the center of the village is a round hut. (In Liberia it is called a *Palaver Hut*. In South Africa it is called a *Ndaba Hut).* The village elders, and the parties to the controversy, meet in the hut and sit on the floor in a circle, facing each other. After some initial small talk, they face up to the problem head-on. They talk things out and settle the problem. When the talk is over, there is a village feast that all attend. And when the feast is over, no person in the village may ever again refer to the problem or controversy. It is past, finished and forgotten! Perhaps we Westerners would do well to refer to our places of worship as *Palaver Huts*!

The Unjust Manager

Luke 16:1–8

Introduction

1. The dilemma that many experience when reading this parable is reflected in comments by C. C. Torrey (*Our Translated Gospels,* New York: Harper, 1936, 5.59):

   > This passage brings before us a new Jesus, one who seems inclined to compromise with evil. He approves a program of canny self-interest, recommending to his disciples a standard of life which is generally recognized as inferior: "I say to you, gain friends by means of money." This is not the worst of it; he bases the teaching on the story of a shrewd scoundrel who feathered his own nest at the expense of the man who had trusted him; and then appears to say to his disciples, "Let this be your model!"

2. True, the parable of the Unjust Manager is perhaps the most difficult of all the parables in the first three Gospels. To understand it, it is essential to understand the culture that colors the text.

3. The most probable cultural setting for the parable is that of a landed estate with a manager who had authority to carry out the business of the estate for its owner, referred to as the "master" in the text. The master was a man of noble character respected in the community, who cared enough about his wealth to fire a wasteful manager. The debtors were most likely renters who had agreed to pay a fixed amount of produce for the yearly rent. The manager was a salaried official who, in addition, was paid a specific fee by the renter for each contract. He was no doubt making a few extras "under the table," but these amounts were not reflected in the signed bills and were not necessarily exorbitant.

4. The Mishna mentions specifically a fee to be paid by a renter to a manager who draws up rent contracts. In addition to this (judging from modern village customs), the manager will likely receive a little extra from most, if not all, of his employer's renters. A token amount is considered legitimate and honorable. At feast time, harvest time, and at other important social occasions, he will likely expect some gratuity from them. He is criticized only if his demands are unreasonable.

5. The community must be considered part of the cast in the parable. The Middle Eastern peasant always thinks and acts as part of his community, not as an individual isolated from it. The involvement of the general public is first implied in verse 1, where we are told, "Charges were brought to him." We are

1 2
4 3

© H.N. Wendt

Parables Unit 8-1

not told who brought these charges. Even if these were only fellow servants, clearly a wider circle of people was involved than just the master, the manager and the debtors.

The Parable

Frame 1, Luke 16:1: *Jesus said to the disciples, "There was a rich man who had a manager.*

The disciples are the primary audience. In verse 1 they are addressed specifically, but Luke suggests that the Pharisees are to be included among the listeners, for in verse 14 they, too, heard "all these things."

Frame 2, Luke 16:1: *And charges were brought to him that this man was squandering his property.*

Frame 3, Luke 16:2: *So he summoned him and said to him, 'What is this that I hear about you? Give me an accounting of your management, because you cannot be my manager any longer.'*

---

1. The manager is summoned and addressed with the first question, 16:2. Literally translated, the question is, "What this I hear about you" (with no verb "is"). The word order is Semitic, idiomatic and forceful. The implication is, "I have been hearing for a long time, and I am still hearing, a steady stream of things about you." It is the stock formula that a master usually uses in such a context. A servant may not know how much his master knows and may be frightened into divulging information the master does not have. However, when the manager, intelligent man that he is, is asked a specific question by his master, he does not respond. His silence throughout the interview is very significant in the Oriental context.

2. The master then breaks the silence with the ultimatum, "Give me an accounting of your management," 16:2. Two important questions must be answered at this point. *First*: Is the manager fired now or later? And *second*: Is the manager asked to "surrender the account books" or to "get the accounts in order"?

3. The first question is problematic. When dealing with the debtors, the manager acts as if he is not yet fired. In verse 3 he says, "My master is taking the position away from me." He then talks about the time "when I am dismissed as manager." At the same time, the present tense of the verb (i.e. "You *cannot be* my manager any longer") indicates that he is fired on the spot.

4. In the conservative village today, a manager is always fired on the spot. The owner is afraid of exactly the kind of thing that happens in this parable. If the rascal has time, he will embezzle more.

5. The manager in the parable is notified that he can no longer serve as manager. Thus, legally his authority as an agent is immediately canceled. At the same time, because word of his dismissal is not out, his dismissal is in progress and he still has some room to maneuver until he turns in the account books.

6. The manager is ordered to turn in the account books. It can be argued that the phrase means "surrender the account books." (In the modern village, a manager in such circumstances is always asked to surrender the books, never to balance the accounts.) The master knows that the manager has the skill to falsify the accounts and so make them of debatable value in establishing the manager's guilt or innocence.

7. The listener/reader of the parable expects the manager to be silent after the first question. But after the manager is told, "You're fired; turn in the books!", the listener/reader expects a classic debate in which the manager protests his innocence. There are many standard ploys he can use to try to defend himself and blame everybody else, including the master himself.

8. But, to the amazement of all, the manager is again silent. He takes his leave of the master having offered no defense. By his silence, the manager is indirectly affirming at least the following:

   a. I am guilty.
   b. The master knows the truth; he knows I am guilty.
   c. This master expects obedience; disobedience brings judgment.
   d. I cannot get my job back by offering a series of excuses.

9. The manager does not reflect on how he can get his job back. He focuses all his energy toward the future. He now speaks—not with the master, but on his way to get the accounts.

10. The manager has discovered something about his master that is supremely significant. Though the master could have tried and jailed him, he fired him but did not jail him. He did not even scold him! The master has been unusually merciful toward him. Thus, in one scene, this manager has experienced two aspects of his master's nature. *First*, he is a master who expects obedience and acts in judgment on disobedient servants. *Second*, he is a master who shows unusual mercy and generosity even to a dishonest manager.

Frame 4, Luke 16:3: Then the manager said to himself, 'What will I do, now that my master is taking the position away from me? I am not strong enough to dig, and I am ashamed to beg.

---

1. The manager wrestles with his crisis: "When I am out of a job, what will I do about housing and food? I must find a solution! I must get another job!" Remarkably, he considers digging. An educated man in authority is not expected to consider manual labor. He will reject this as a possibility because it is beneath his dignity. Surprisingly, his only reason is his physical weakness. He also rejects begging. This, likewise, is to his credit in a society that accepts begging as a legitimate, although despised, profession.

2. His problem is not just his next roof and meal. Because he has been dismissed for wasting his master's property, who will hire him? He needs to create a situation that will change this devastating public image.

Frame 5, Luke 16:4: I have decided what to do so that, when I am dismissed as manager, people may welcome me into their homes.'

---

1. A plan pops into the manager's scheming mind. Listeners/readers are not told what the plan is; rather, as in all good drama, they watch it unfold.

2. Because the manager was legally powerless from the moment he was notified of his dismissal, he realizes that he must act quickly and decisively—before anyone in the community finds out that he has been fired, before he hands over the account books, and before he is out of office. If the debtors have any way of knowing that deception is involved in any plan the manager sets before them, they will not cooperate. If a lesser servant enters the room and announces that the steward is fired, the scheme fails. The renters may entertain suspicions (the community knows him; cf. 16:1), but as long as they have no knowledge they can and will cooperate.

3. Furthermore, the manager must finish implementing his plan before the master finds out what he is doing. This fact is crucial to the story.

4. The goal of the manager's plan is to place people under obligation to him, so that when he is out of a job, they will feel constrained to provide him with lodging and food, even if only on a short-term basis. The plan is to do the tenants a "favor," so that they in turn will do him a favor.

Frame 6, Luke 16:5–7: *⁵So, summoning his master's debtors one by one, he asked the first, 'How much do you owe my master?' ⁶He answered, 'A hundred jugs of olive oil.' He said to him, 'Take your bill, sit down quickly, and make it fifty.' ⁷Then he asked another, 'And how much do you owe?' He replied, 'A hundred containers of wheat.' He said to him, 'Take your bill and make it eighty.'*

---

1. At the heart of the manager's plan is the decision to risk everything on the quality of mercy he has already experienced from his master. If he fails, he will certainly go to jail. If he succeeds, he will be a hero in the community.

2. He "summons" the debtors. Only if he were still in authority would he have the right to send out lesser servants and summon these relatively rich and thereby important men to come and see him (their wealth is evident from the large rents owed). The assumption of such a summoning would naturally be that the manager has some important message to relay to them from the master. As it turns out, this is exactly what the manager wants them to assume. It is not harvest time. The amounts of the bills are set and outstanding, but not yet due.

3. He calls the debtors in one by one because he does not want them talking to one another and asking too many questions. He is in too much of a hurry for titles. The debtors are not greeted with even "Friend" or "Sir." To the first he says specifically, "Write quickly." To the second he says almost rudely, "And you."

4. When the tenants arrive, the manager takes the bills from his drawer, cupboard or file, observes the amount, and asks each debtor how much it is. The debtor affirms the amount written. The manager then announces a reduction that, in each case, amounts to about 500 denarii. That the values of the two reductions are roughly equivalent is another indication of his haste. It is much easier to subtract 500 denarii worth from each bill than to debate the fairness of a percentage with each debtor.

5. From the haste of the manager and from modern and ancient custom, it is clear that the debtors assume the bill-changing to be legitimate. *First*, the debtors are led to believe that the manager is still in authority. After all, the manager summons them. The manager says, "How much do you owe *my master*?" He directly asserts that he is still employed. *Second*, they assume that the master has authorized the bills and that the manager has talked him into it.

6. The manager asks the debtors to make the changes in their own handwriting. They accept. The amounts reach to fifty percent. We must assume that the debtors are confident that the master has approved. If there is any doubt about this, they will not cooperate. The risk is too great. If they know or could have known, and then cooperate, they will be breaking faith with the master in a very serious way, and the master will no longer rent land to them—a significant cultural factor. Throughout the parable, the tenants are assumed to be upright citizens of the local community. They cannot be viewed as partners-in-crime.

7. The manager naturally takes credit for having arranged the reductions. He need say little or nothing. The bills are not due. These sudden reductions come, as it were, "out of the blue." The manager may quietly let it be known, "I talked the old gentleman into it." We can easily reconstruct the kind of small talk that would have taken place during the bill changing. After all, he, the manager, was in the fields day after day. He knew that the rain was bad, the sun hot, and the worms active. The manager thus achieves the position of a factory foreman who has arranged a generous Christmas bonus for all of the workers. The bonus itself is from the owners. But the foreman is praised for having talked the owners into granting it. The last part of this assumption is also inescapable. The manager will not carry out a plan that does not reflect to his credit in a significant way. There would be no point in doing so.

Frame 7

1. After meeting with the tenants, the manager finishes his daring plan by gathering up the freshly changed accounts and delivering them to his master. The master looks at them and reflects on his alternatives.

2. A great round of celebrations is under way in the village! The villagers are praising the master as the most noble and generous man that ever rented land in their district. When he goes among them, they greet him warmly and bow to him!

3. The master can do one of two things. *First option:* He can go to the debtors, tell them that it is all a mistake, that the manager has been dismissed and his actions are null and void. But if the master does this, the villagers' joy will turn to anger. They will curse him for his stinginess. He cannot afford to lose face in the community. He is trapped!

Frame 8, Luke 16:8: And the master commended the dishonest manager because he had acted shrewdly."

1. *Second option:* The master can keep silent, accept the praise that is already being showered on him, and allow the clever manager to ride high on the wave of popular enthusiasm. He chooses this option!

2. The master is a generous man. To be generous is a primary quality of a nobleman in the East. He reflects for a moment and then turns to the manager and says, "You are a smart fellow. You certainly know how to take care of yourself—and your future!" He did not jail the manager earlier. He does not jail him now.

3. In summary, the manager is praised for his skillfulness in self-preservation. He is sensitive to the hopelessness of his situation. He is aware of the one source of salvation, namely, the generosity of his master.

Concluding comments

1. As an Oriental story, the parable builds to a climax awaiting the owner's response at the end of the parable. Verse 8a is the climax of the parable.

2. Many have worried over how Jesus could use a dishonest man as an example. This need not trouble us. The Middle Eastern peasant at the bottom of the economic ladder finds such a parable pure delight. Nothing pleases him more than a story in which some David kills a Goliath.

3. Even so, there is an unusual feature to this story. The storyteller in the East always has a series of stories about the clever fellow who won out over the "Mister Big" of his community. The remarkable feature of this parable is that the manager is criticized as "unrighteous" and called a "son of darkness." The average Oriental storyteller would not feel any compulsion to add such a corrective to this type of story. Though the Western listener/reader is surprised at the use of a dishonest man as a hero, the Eastern listener/reader is surprised that such a hero is criticized.

4. Jesus made use of unsavory characters in several other parables: the unjust judge, the neighbor who does not want to be bothered in the night, and the man who pockets someone else's treasure by buying his field. The parable of the unjust manager is only the most outstanding example of a class of parables.

5. In three of the four cases listed in 4. above, Jesus uses the rabbinic principle of "from the light to the heavy," which means generally, "How much more?" That is, if this widow got what she wanted from this kind of judge (18:1–9), how much more would you get from God? If this man got bread in the night from this neighbor (11:5–7), how much more would you get from God? If this dishonest steward solved his problem by relying on the mercy of his master to solve his crisis, how much more will God help you in your crisis when you trust His mercy?

6. Verse 8b reads: "The children of this generation are more shrewd in dealing with their own generation than the children of light."

    This verse, which is part of the original telling of the parable, provides the necessary corrective to the approval of the unjust manager. He is praised for his wisdom in knowing where his salvation lay, not for his dishonesty.

7. The entire parable offers insights into the nature of God, into the crises that the kingdom brings to the sinner, and into the only hope for humanity's salvation. Its message can be summarized as follows:

    > God [the master] is a God of judgment and mercy. Because of his evil, man [the manager] is caught in the crisis of the coming of the kingdom. Excuses will avail the manager nothing. This clever rascal was wise enough to place his total trust in the quality of mercy experienced at the beginning of the story. That trust was vindicated.

    > Disciples need the same kind of wisdom. Their only option is to entrust everything to the unfailing mercy of their generous Heavenly Master who, they can be confident, will accept to pay the price for their salvation.

The Judge and the Widow

Luke 18:1–8

Introduction

1. Luke 18:1–14 contains two parables: (1) The Judge and the Widow (18:1–8) and (2) The Pharisee and the Publican, 18:9–14. The opening verse to each explains their respective emphases:

> Then Jesus told them a parable about their need to pray always and not to lose heart.
>
> *—Luke 18:1*

> Jesus also told this parable to some who trusted in themselves that they were righteous and regarded others with contempt.
>
> *—Luke 18:9*

2. Jesus' audience consists of the disciples, Luke 17:22, 18:1. He tells them the parable of the Judge and the Widow to encourage them to persist in prayer. They are to remember at all times that the God to whom they pray is the Creator of all, the One who began and directs history—and is still involved in it. They are to trust God, and to seek Him when their confidence is wavering and when He seems far away.

Frame 1 of the illustration points to the nature of the prayer life Jesus wishes people to pursue as they pray "in His name," John 14:13,14; 15:16; 16:23,24,26.

---

1. To pray "in Jesus' name" is not merely to use a divine formula that guarantees the granting of any petition, no matter what it might be.

2. The term "in Jesus' name" is one of *identification*, not *manipulation*. In short, Christians are to pray for the things Jesus prayed for. We never read of Jesus praying to be given any material goods or objects. He prayed only that He might know and do His Father's will, no matter what that might entail for Him, Luke 22:42.

3. If Jesus lived the life of a servant-without-limit, His people are to pray that they might be enlightened and empowered to reflect His mind and manner in all they do.

4. The illustration shows Jesus, the Servant-King, complete with basin and towel, preparing to wash His disciples' feet. If the Savior and Lord of the universe dedicated His life to living that way, then those who claim allegiance to Him are to do the same.

5. The "good gift" the Father wishes to give His children is that of the Holy Spirit (*dove*). However, the Holy Spirit's sole purpose is to make Jesus known and perpetuate His ministry. Those who persist in asking, searching and knocking in relation to the Spirit's desires for them will receive what they ask for, Luke 11:9,10.

The Parable

The first verse of the parable itself introduces the judge, the next verse the widow, the next verse the judge, and the next verse the widow.

Frame 2, Luke 18:2: "In a certain city there was a judge who neither feared God nor had respect for people.

The judge's problem is not failure to respect someone higher than he. It is his inability to sense the evil of his actions in the presence of One who should make him feel ashamed. The whole world may cry "Shame!" to no effect, for this judge has no fear of God. The cry of "For God's sake" is meaningless in his ears, as is also the cry, "For this destitute widow's sake." The only way to influence him is to resort to bribery!

Frame 3, Luke 18:3: In that city there was a widow who kept coming to him and saying, 'Grant me justice against my opponent.'

---

1. Throughout the Old Testament, widows are viewed as symbols of those who are innocent, powerless and oppressed, Exodus 22:22–23; Deuteronomy 10:18, 24:17, 27:19; Job 22:9, 24:3,21; Psalm 68:5; Isaiah 10:2. Isaiah 1:17 calls on the rulers and people to "plead for the widow," and in verse 23 the prophet writes:

> Everyone loves a bribe and runs after gifts.
>   They do not defend the orphan,
>   and the widow's cause does not come before them.

2. On the basis of this passage, the Jewish legal tradition required that the suit of an orphan must always be heard first, and that of a widow next. A widow was always vulnerable and there were always many ready to prey on her. Obviously, this woman's legal rights were being violated; her cry is for justice and protection, not vengeance. However, she is in no position to compel, or to buy, the legal services that she needs.

3. Most likely, the issue is money, for, according to the Talmud, a qualified scholar could decide money cases sitting alone. Apparently the judge does not want to serve her—possibly because she is not in any position to pay a bribe. Perhaps the judge prefers to favor her adversary—who perhaps has paid a bribe.

Frame 3, Luke 18:4: *For a while he refused; but later he said to himself, 'Though I have no fear of God and no respect for anyone...*

Initially, the judge states that he feels no sense of obligation to God or responsibility to humanity.

Frame 4, Luke 18:5: *...yet because this widow keeps bothering me, I will grant her justice, so that she may not wear me out by continually coming.'"*

Eventually, the judge finds the woman overly bothersome and fears she might wear him out. Though he uses a prizefighting term ("wear me out") for giving someone a blow under the eye in a fight, there is no suggestion that he fears the woman might get physically violent. She can shout all kinds of verbal insults, but if she gets physically violent she will be forcibly removed and not allowed to return. The judge's fear is rather that the woman will never give up, and that she will give him so many verbal blows to the head that he will finish up with a gigantic headache!

Frame 5: *The widow gets a hearing, a decision in her favor, and goes on her way rejoicing.*

The Point of the Parable

If this woman gets her needs met, how much more will the pious get their needs met—the pious who pray, not to a harsh judge, but to a loving Father. They can rest assured that their petitions are heard and granted. God will hear and act in their best interests. The parable is an appeal to persistence in prayer.

Cultural Background

In the last century, a Western traveler witnessed a scene in Iraq that gives us the wider picture behind the first of these two parables. He wrote:

> It was in the ancient city of Nisibis, in Mesopotamia. Immediately on entering the gate of the city, on one side stood the prison with its barred windows, through which the prisoners thrust their arms and begged for alms. Opposite was a large open hall, the court of justice of the place. On a slightly raised dais at the further end sat the *Kadi* or judge, half buried in cushions. Round him squatted various secretaries and other notables. The populace crowded into the rest of the hall, a dozen voices clamoring at once, each claiming that his cause should be the first heard. The more prudent litigants joined not in the fray, but held whispered communications with the secretaries, passing bribes, euphemistically called fees, into the hands of one or another. When the greed of the underlings was satisfied, one of them would whisper to the *Kadi*, who would promptly call such and such a case. It seemed to be ordinarily taken for granted that judgment would go for the litigant who had bribed highest. But meantime a poor woman on the skirts of the crowd perpetually interrupted the proceedings with loud cries for justice. She was sternly bidden to be silent, and reproachfully told that she came there every day. "And so I will," she cried out, "till the *Kadi* hears me." At length, at the end of a suit, the judge impatiently demanded, "What does that woman want?"

Her story was soon told. Her only son had been taken for a soldier, and she was alone, and could not till her piece of ground; yet the tax-gatherer had forced her to pay the impost, from which a lone widow could be exempt. The judge asked a few questions, and said, "Let her be exempt." Thus her perseverance was rewarded. Had she had money to fee a clerk, she might have been excused long before.

—H.B. Tristram, *Eastern Customs in Bible Lands*
(London: Hodder and Stoughton, 1984, p. 228f.)

Though many have referred to this account when analyzing the parable, a key element in Jesus' parable and Tristram's account has gone unnoticed. Ordinarily women in the Middle East do not go to court. Court, with its shouting and pushing and shoving, is considered a man's world. The Jewish tractate *Shebuoth* states that it is not usual for a woman to go to court, for a woman is modest, and stays within her home as much as possible. In the light of this, it would follow that the widow in the parable lives alone, and has no men in an extended family to speak for her. She is a widow in a man's world, and has neither money nor powerful friends.

Dr. Kenneth Bailey tells the following story:

> During the Lebanese civil war of 1975–76, a Palestinian peasant woman of my acquaintance was caught in a tragedy. Her cousin disappeared. He was assumed to be kidnapped by one of the many armed groups fighting in the city of Beirut. The entire extended family searched in vain for him or his body. He was the only son of his widowed mother and was not a member of any paramilitary group. In desperation the family sent a delegation of three peasant *women* to the political/military leader of the leftist forces in the area where he had disappeared. The man they went to see was an internationally known powerful military and political figure. These three women shouted their way into an audience with him and, once there, flung a torrent of hard words in his face. The entire scene was vividly described to me by my peasant friend the following day. I specifically asked, "What would have happened if the men of your family had said such things to this man?" With raised eyebrows and a shake of her head she answered, "O, they would have been killed at once." Tristram heard "...a dozen voices clamoring at once, each claiming that his cause should be the first heard." Thus *many* people were shouting. How did the *widow* get attention? Obviously her shouting was different from the others. In traditional society in the Middle East women are generally powerless in a man's world. But at the same time, they are respected and honored. Men can be mistreated in public, but not women. Women can scream at a public figure and nothing will happen to them. In the case of my Palestinian friend, the family had *deliberately* sent the women because they could express openly their sense of hurt and betrayal in language guaranteed to evoke a response. The men could not say the same thing and stay alive. This same background is reflected in the rest of the parable.

—*Through Peasant Eyes*, p. 135

Old Testament Background

1. Several Old Testament passages are "required reading" when probing Jesus' parable, namely 2 Chronicles 19:4–6 and Amos 2:6,7; 5:10–13. In His well-known writings on the parables, Edersheim makes reference to judges who were quite corrupt, and called "robber-judges" rather than "judges of

prohibitions"—a description that involves a play on words in Hebrew. The Talmud speaks of judges who were willing to pervert justice for a dish of meat (B.T. Baba Kamma 114a).

2. While English versions generally translate to suggest that the judge did not regard or respect people, the real point is that he is not *ashamed* before people. The culture of the Middle East is, to a remarkable degree, a shame/pride culture where the focus is not so much on avoiding what is *wrong*, but on avoiding what is *shameful*. Still today, it is quite terrible to be able to say of someone, "He does not feel shame!" The person referred to lacks an inner sense of what constitutes a good act or a shameful act; he cannot be shamed.

3. Jeremiah makes vivid reference to wise men who lack shame (8:9) and have lost the ability to blush, 8:12. In His parable about a landlord seeking rent, Jesus makes reference to rebellious tenants who treat the landlord's messengers shamefully, Mark 12:1–12; Luke 20:9–19.

Jesus and Sirach

1. Sirach 35:14–20 is a prototype of Luke 18:1–8. It reads:

> He will not ignore the supplication of the orphan,
> > or the widow when she pours out her complaint.
> Do not the tears of a widow run down her cheek
> > as she cries out against the one who causes them to fall?
> The one whose service is pleasing to the Lord will be accepted,
> > and his prayers will reach to the clouds.
> The prayer of the humble pierces the clouds
> > and it will not rest until it reaches its goal;
> It will not desist until the Most High responds,
> > and does justice for the righteous, and executes judgment.
> Indeed, the Lord will not delay and like a warrior will not be patient
> > until he crushes the loins of the unmerciful.

2. When we compare this passage with Luke 18:1–8, we see what Jesus borrowed, what He transformed, and what He left out. The *similarities* are:

    a. Each begins with prayer in general. Then, after an illustration, each moves on to discuss the specific topic of justice for the righteous in the face of oppression.

    b. Both go from the light to the heavy.

3. The *similarities with a difference* are:

    a. Both describe a widow crying for help. In Jesus' parable, the widow persists in her actions. Sirach switches from the widow to a humble man who will not be consoled until he has an answer. Thus, Jesus makes more of persistence, while Sirach shifts to a male figure.

    b. Though both refer to God's patience, Sirach says God is not patient with the ungodly, while Jesus says He is.

    c. Both discuss vindication of the righteous. Sirach speaks of justice for the righteous and vengeance for the unrighteous, while Jesus makes no reference to the latter.

d.   Each uses a concrete illustration: the plight of a widow.

4.   The *points of complete dissimilarity* are:

   a.   According to Sirach, the way to get prayers answered is to render a service pleasing to the Lord. Those who do so are accepted and their prayers reach the clouds. These notions are not found in Jesus' parable.

   b.   Jesus' parable introduces a sharper cutting edge in that it uses the figure of an unjust judge to represent God—a bold and risky image!

5.   Though Jesus makes use of Sirach's words, He transforms them and omits some of their detail. The closing words of Jesus' parable confront us with a question: Do we show a faith as persistent as that of the nagging widow?

The Implications of 18:6–8

1.   The final sentence of the parable seems to indicate an uneasiness about the quality of faith in the believing community. It seems to suggest that many do not exhibit the will to endure what the woman in the parable exhibited—and might lose heart and, in the process, also faith. The question is: What is meant by the term "delay" used, for example, in the NRSV translation of verse 7?

2.   The word "delay" here translates the Greek word *makrothumeo* (verb), one of the three great words the New Testament uses for "showing patience." "Delay" does not do justice to it. The second word for patience is *anoche*—used in Romans 2:4 and 3:26. It denotes God's divine forbearance in passing over sin. The third is *upomone*, which refers to the patience of a sufferer—above all, to the patience of Jesus on the cross.

3.   The rabbis provide a marvelous illustration of *makrothumia* (noun), long suffering. They tell of a king who wondered where to station his troops. He decided to locate them at some distance from the capital, so that on the occasion of civil disobedience, it would take some time for them to march in. In that interim, the rebels would have opportunity to come to their senses and "So, it is argued, God keeps His wrath at a distance to give Israel time to repent" (T.W. Manson, *Sayings*, 308; c.f. P.T. *Tannith*, 11.65b).

4.   At the same time, according to Sirach 35:19–20, God has no *makrothumia* toward the Gentiles.

> And the Lord will not delay,
>   nor will he be slow to anger [*makrothumia*] with them,
> till He crushes the loins of the unmerciful,
>   and repays vengeance on the nations.

5.   Luke offers no sharp attack on the Gentiles. Instead, he closes with the wish that the *faithful* will continue in faith, and that the Son of Man will find faith on earth when He comes.

6.   Only the first two sections of Luke 18:7 should be read as a question. Bailey translates as follows:

Shall not God make vindication for His elect,
    the ones crying to Him day and night?
Also He is slow to anger over them.
    I say to you that He shall make vindication for them speedily.

7. The general thrust is that God will indeed vindicate His elect who cry to Him day and night. However, those same elect are sinners—not sinless saints. If God were not willing to put aside His anger over sin, they could not approach Him in prayer. They dare not call out for vindication lest the Day of the Lord be a day of darkness and not light, Amos 5:18–20. The act of seeking vindication does not make people righteous, nor does a righteous cause produce righteous people.

8. God's children can pray to Him day and night without fear only because God has put His anger aside. God vindicates His people, even though they have sinned, only because of His great *makrothumia*— because He has put aside His wrath and shows mercy to them. God's slowness to anger and rich grace kindle faith within people and inspire them to pray with a fervor that moves mountains.

9. Jesus tells the parable under review while approaching Jerusalem, Luke 19:28. The passion is rapidly approaching. Jesus' opponents are preparing to deliver their final act of opposition to Him. They will soon send Him to a cross. Will God vindicate Jesus? Yes, God will vindicate His Son who also prays to Him day and night, but that vindication will be seen in resurrection and will come by way of a cross.

10. For centuries, Islam has had difficulty with the concept of Jesus' crucifixion. Muslims see Jesus merely as a great prophet. In the Psalms, God says, "Touch not my anointed ones; do my prophets no harm," Psalm 105:15. In light of this verse, Islam asks, "Where is God's vindication of His prophet in the passion narratives? How can the story of the cross be true?" Hence, Islam rewrites the story of the cross to suggest that not Jesus, but a substitute, went to the cross. But the question is valid: Where is Jesus' vindication? Jesus' vindication is declared by the empty tomb! Even so, that vindication went via Golgotha.

11. Some believe that the final verse (Luke 18:8) points only to events connected with possibly a distant return and final appearance of Jesus. However, it might well point to Jesus' immediate ministry. The question is: Is God going to vindicate Jesus and the little band of fearful believers that has cast their lot with Him? T.W. Manson points out that the disciples' election was to service and not to privilege:

> They are not the pampered darlings of Providence, but the *corps d'elite* in the army of the living God. Because they are what they are, they are foredoomed to suffering at the hands of the wicked; and in many cases the seal of election is martyrdom.
>
> —*Sayings*, 307

12. The parable assured the disciples that God would vindicate Jesus and the disciples—and do so quickly. It assures us that, though we can expect to encounter opposition in this world, we need not fear. God has put His anger far away and He hears us. We must trust God at every step along the way, and pray constantly and zealously. We can pray with confidence, for in our prayer life we do not appeal to a disgruntled judge, but to a gracious forgiving Father who will vindicate His elect and do so quickly.

The Pharisee
and
the Tax Collector

Luke 18:9–14

Introduction

1. The opening verse (18:9) states:

    > Jesus also told this parable to some who trusted in themselves that they were
    > righteous and regarded others with contempt.

    The "some" were the Pharisees. The "others" were people such as tax collectors—and humanity at large.

2. In the Temple of Jesus' day, a lamb was sacrificed at dawn for the sins of the people. A second similar sacrifice was offered at three in the afternoon. When the time came for the burning of incense, this was thought to be an appropriate time for private prayer because, by this time in the service, the sacrifice of the lamb had covered the sins of Israel and thus the way to God was open. The faithful could now approach God personally.

3. It seems likely that the two men in the parable went to the Temple to be present for either a dawn or mid-afternoon ritual as mentioned above. Others were obviously present, for the Pharisee stood by himself (away from others), and the tax collector stood far off (from others). Furthermore, the tax collector's reference to an "atonement" in his prayer makes it all the more likely that either the regular morning or afternoon sacrifice is being offered, with people present.

4. Those who kept the law strictly thought of themselves as *haberim* ("associates"), and of all others as *am-ha-aretz* ("people [of] the land"). For a Pharisee, the most obvious candidate for inclusion among the *am-ha-aretz* would be a tax collector.

5. The self-understanding of each man is revealed in his respective prayer.

    a. The Pharisee's prayer is much longer than that of the tax collector. As the Pharisee presents his case to God (18:11,12), we see that he understands himself as a strict observer of the law.

© H.N. Wendt

b. Though we also initially see the tax collector (considered a breaker of the law and a traitor to the nation!) through the Pharisee's eyes (18:11b), we later see the tax collector's own view of himself, 18:13.

The Parable

Frame 1, Luke 18:10: "Two men..., one a Pharisee and the other a Publican...

Frame 2, Luke 18:10: ...went up to the Temple to pray.

It would appear the two men go up to the Temple together, and also leave together. It is just possible that when they go up to the Temple, the Pharisee leads; and when they go down from the Temple, the tax collector leads.

Frame 3, Luke 18:11,12: The Pharisee, standing by himself, was praying thus, 'God, I thank you that I am not like other people: thieves, rogues, adulterers, or even like this tax collector. I fast twice a week; I give a tenth of all my income.'

---

1. When the Pharisee prays, he stands apart from others—for several reasons. The *am-haaretz* did not observe the Pharisaic rules of cleanliness nor did they set aside tithes—and the Pharisee specifically mentions the paying of tithes. While incense was being offered up, all considered "unclean" were ushered to the Eastern Gate and made to stand there. Perhaps the Pharisees is asking himself, "Why did they not take this tax collector along with them?"

2. Though the Pharisee stands by himself, he does not talk to himself for *he wants to be heard!* In praying aloud, he preaches to the "lesser breed" around him. He wants them to get a good look at a truly "righteous" man (himself!), and "graciously" offers them a few words of judgment plus some instruction in righteousness.

3. In Jewish piety, to pray was to thank and praise God for all His good gifts, and to pray for needs. The Pharisee does neither. He merely boasts of his own self-achieved righteousness, and indulges in self-congratulation. His prayer goes from bad to worse as he makes reference to thieves, rogues, adulterers, the unjust and the tax collector. (It is likely that the Pharisee constructs the list that he does because he understands each detail to apply to the tax collector.)

4. The first two words in the Pharisee's list can be translated as *thieves and rogues*, or *rogues and swindlers*. The tax farmers of the Roman empire were traditionally known as extortioners and swindlers. The third word, "adulterers," is thrown in by the Pharisee for good measure—the older son does a similar thing in Luke 15:30. The Pharisee is presuming something!

5. In listing his own virtues and attacking others, the Pharisee shreds his own spirituality. His so-called prayer is not a prayer—but a ruthless, public attack on a fellow worshiper at a great altar. It is based on preconceived notions and molded by the Pharisee's arrogant self-righteousness, which he then proudly displays with, "I fast twice a week; I give a tenth of all my income."

6. The Law stipulated that people should fast on the Day of Atonement, Leviticus 25:29; Numbers 39:7. However, the Pharisee fasts twice each week—a practice confined to certain circles of the Pharisees and their disciples.

7. Tithes were levied on grain, wine and oil, Leviticus 27:30; Numbers 18:27; Deuteronomy 12:17, 14:13. But this Pharisee congratulates himself on the fact that he not only keeps the Law but exceeds its demands; he pays tithes on everything! He obviously was not familiar with Amos 4:4.

8. The Pharisee, then, stands aloof (lest he be defiled by the "unrighteous" around him), congratulates himself, offers scathing criticism of a tax collector nearby, and finally brags of not only having kept the law but of having exceeded its demands.

Frame 4, Luke 18:13: But the tax collector, standing far off, would not even look up to heaven, but was beating his breast and saying, 'God, be merciful to me, a sinner!'

---

1. The turning point in the parable comes in 18:13. The image the Pharisee has of the tax collector is different from the reality. The tax collector stands "far off," for he does not consider himself worthy to stand before God's altar or near the assembled worshipers.

2. The accepted posture for prayer was to cross the hands over the chest and keep the eyes cast down. However, the tax collector does not keep his hands still; he uses them to beat on his chest in rapid succession.

    People still do this today in villages all across the Middle East—from Iraq to Egypt— to express extreme anguish or intense anger. The practice is never mentioned in the Old Testament, and is mentioned only twice in the New Testament, both times in Luke; see also Luke 23:48.

3. In his prayer, the tax collector uses a word that refers to the atonement sacrifice. He is not offering a general prayer for God's mercy, but yearns for the benefit of an atonement. He has watched priests perform a number of rituals in the name of the people, slaughter and cut up the sacrificial lamb, burn incense, pronounce a blessing with outstretched hands, and put God's name on the children of Israel. He has seen and heard the clash of cymbals, the blasts on the trumpets, the reading of the Psalms, the singing of the choir of Levites, and the final prostration of the people. He sees and hears it all—and longs to be part of it all. In deep remorse, he strikes his chest and cries out in repentance and hope, "O God, let it be for me! Make an atonement for me, a sinner!" He desires that the great atonement sacrifice he has just witnessed might apply also to him.

Frame 5, Luke 18:14: I tell you, this man went down to his home justified rather than the other; for all who exalt themselves will be humbled, and all who humble themselves will be exalted."

---

1. The incident begins with two men going up to the Temple together. It ends with two men leaving the Temple together. The tax collector is the one justified in God's presence. The self-righteous Pharisee returns home unjustified.

2. In the parable's conclusion, Jesus states, "For all who exalt themselves will be humbled, but all who humble themselves will be exalted," 18:14b; see also Matthew 18:4; 23:12; Luke 14:11; 1 Peter 5:6. His words affirm that only the humble will be exalted.

3. The introduction of the parable speaks of those who elevate themselves and consider themselves righteous, while they humiliate and despise others. It ends by pointing out that those who exalt themselves will be humbled, and those who humble themselves will be exalted. The tax collector has been delivered, redeemed and exalted—actions that only God can perform.

4. Through the parable, Jesus proclaimed to His hearers that righteousness was a gift of God made possible by means of the atonement sacrifice. It was received by those who, in humility, approached God not as saints but as sinners. It was received by those who trusted, not in their own righteousness, but in God's grace.

Obviously, Paul's teaching of justification by grace, through faith in Christ crucified and risen, has its roots in Jesus' teaching.

The Cultural Setting

1. The scribes and Pharisees held that there was a particular kind of uncleanness that was contracted by sitting on, riding on, or even leaning against something unclean. This uncleanness was called *midras*-uncleanness. The Mishnah states, "For Pharisees the clothes of an *am-ha-aretz* count as suffering *midras*-uncleanness" (Mishna, *Hagigah 2:7*, Danby 214). Little wonder that the Pharisee stood apart from worshipers. Even if a Pharisee brushed against a tax collector or an *am-ha-aretz* he would sustain *midras*-uncleanness. Because his state of cleanness is too important to permit any compromise, the Pharisee stands aloof from those gathered around the altar. For him, his physical isolation makes an important statement. He stands *aloof* because he believes others are not worthy to be in his presence. The tax collector, on the other hand, stands *alone* because he believes he is not worthy to be in the presence of others.

2. The great rabbi Hillel offered the following advice:

> Keep not aloof from the congregation and trust not in thyself until the day of thy death, and judge not thy fellow until thou art thyself come to his place.
> —*Mishna,* Pirke Aboth *2:5, Danby, 448*

3. The remarkable feature of Luke's references to people beating on their chest is that they apply to both men and women, 18:13, 23:48. In the Middle East today, the practice is characteristic of women—not men. Bailey reports that, during twenty years of observation in the Middle East, he found only one occasion in which Middle Eastern *men* are accustomed to beat on their chests—at the *'Ashura* ritual of Shiite Islam. This ritual is an enactment of the murder of Hussein, the son of Ali (the son-in-law of the prophet of Islam). The murder scene is dramatically presented and the devotees lacerate their shaved heads with knives and razors in a demonstration of extreme anguish as they recollect this community-forming event. At this ritual, *men* beat on their chests. Women customarily beat on their chests at funerals, but men do not. For men it is a gesture of extreme sorrow and anguish, and it is almost never used.

4. Why beat on the *chest*? An early Jewish commentary on Ecclesiastes 7:2 states:

> R. Mana said: And the living will lay it to his heart: these are the righteous who set their death over against their heart; and why do they beat upon their heart? as though to say, "All is there."
> —Midrash Rabbah, *Eccl. VII,2,5, Sonc., 177*

The meaning is that the righteous beat their heart as the source of evil longing. Similarly, in Matthew 15:19, Jesus says, "Out of the heart come evil intentions, murder, adultery, fornication, theft, false witness, slander."

The Pharisee in the parable viewed the tax collector as one without merit and hope before God. The story that follows describes vividly the biblical truth in relation to salvation:

In "I Married You," Walter Trobisch recounts experiences during a visit to Africa during which be gave a series of lectures on marriage and related matters. During this particular stay in Africa, Trobisch was driven around by a driver called Maurice. Maurice wanted to marry, but insisted that when he did, it would be to a virgin—a condition not easily met. Early one morning, during the close of his stay in Africa, Trobisch woke with a start and felt a strong inner compulsion to go to a bridge in the city. Maurice saw to it that he got to the bridge in a hurry. When the two men arrived, they saw a woman standing in the middle of the bridge, looking down into the swiftly-flowing flooded stream below. She was deeply distressed, and preparing to commit suicide.

Trobisch knew the woman and her background. He had already been trying to help her. Her life had been one of moral and spiritual chaos. She was tormented by the memory of her many illicit love affairs and her numerous other gross sins. She felt she could not bear the burden of these memories any longer. However, Trobisch was able to persuade her not to kill herself, and eventually God used him, and others, to bring her to a joyous faith in Jesus as her Savior and Lord.

While Trobisch was talking to the woman on the bridge (her name was Fatma), Maurice remained in the car and prayed. While he prayed, something remarkable happened—of which Trobisch was to learn only later.

Eventually the day arrived when Trobisch and his wife Ingrid left Africa to fly back to Europe. A number of friends came to say farewell to them. Among them was Maurice—with Fatma standing next to him. As the Trobischs left the terminal to board the aircraft, Maurice pushed a letter into Trobisch's hand, asked him to read it only after take-off, and to send him a reply as soon as possible. After the plane reached cruising altitude, Trobisch read the following:

> Walter, when I prayed in the car on the bridge while you were talking to Fatma, a voice came to me as clear as a bell. It said, "This girl with whom Walter is talking will be your wife." It was crazy. I had never seen her before and had no idea who she was, or what she looked like. Could this have been God's voice? Please send me a telegram "Yes," or "No," from the next stop.

Trobisch shared the contents of the letter with his wife and commented, "Poor Maurice. He wanted so much to marry a virgin, and it looks as though he'll finish up with Fatma!" Ingrid thought for a while and eventually responded, "But Walter, Fatma is a virgin now. She is washed in the blood of Jesus. She is without spot, without wrinkle, without blemish—as the bride of Christ. Maurice will marry a virgin!"

The Trobischs sent Maurice a prompt rely: "Yes!"

Though the only authentic thing we humans can offer God is sin, what God offers us freely, and without price, is the full forgiveness of sins through Jesus, crucified, risen and reigning.

Appendix
Questions for Study & Discussion
©H.N. Wendt, 1998

Unit 1

*The Fox, the Funeral,
the Farewell, the Furrow*

Read Luke 9:51–62

---

1. When Jesus tells this parable, where is he going?

2. Why did the Samaritans refuse to welcome Him into their midst?

3. Along the way, Jesus encountered three men, 9:57–62. What did the first volunteer offer to do?

4. How did Jesus respond to him, and what did His response mean?

5. How did the second man respond to Jesus' invitation? Why do people generally empathize with the man's response? What did his response mean?

6. How did Jesus respond to the second man, and what did His response mean?

7. The third man volunteered to follow Jesus, but added a condition. Again, though people generally empathize with the man's condition, what did it imply?

8. What do Jesus' words in 9:62 mean?

9. Read Jesus' predictions of His approaching passion in Mark 8:27–38; 9:31–35; 10:32–45. Each section contains three elements: (1) a prediction by Jesus, (2) confusion on the part of the disciples, and (3) statements by Jesus in which he clarifies what it means to belong to Him and live under Him in His Kingdom.

    a. Discern the three elements in each incident.

    b. Discuss what they imply for us today as we seek to live as Jesus' brothers and sisters.

10. Summarize briefly the message that the parable speaks to us today.

Read Luke 10:25–37

---

1. If you have access to the Apocrypha, read Sirach 12:1–7. What does Sirach say about how God feels toward the "ungodly," and how the righteous should treat them?

2. Read the opening dialogue in 10:25–28.

    a. What question did the lawyer pose?

    b. Why might he have asked it?

    c. How did Jesus handle his question?

3. Why did the lawyer ask the question in 10:29?

4. Jesus might well have responded to his question with a brief answer. Instead, He told the lawyer a story. Why did Jesus respond that way?

5. Why didn't the priest and the Levite help the victim they encountered?

6. Why is it ironic that a Samaritan went to his aid?

7. What risks did the Samaritan take in acting as he did?

8. In telling the parable, Jesus removed all limits as to who the neighbor is, and all limits as to how far we should go in helping that neighbor.

    a. How does the parable make these points?

    b. How and why do people today rationalize ("rational-lies") the limits they place on serving others?

9. Summarize briefly the message the parable speaks to us today.

Read Luke 11:1–8

---

1. What takes place immediately before the telling of this parable, 11:1–4?

2. The man in the parable found himself faced with a problem. What was it?

3. Though we presume that he went to his neighbor's house and knocked on the door, where does the text say he knocked? How did he get his neighbor's attention?

4. Why did the man ask for bread? Didn't he have any food in his home?

5. How would you have felt had you been the neighbor to whom the would-be host called out?

6. How valid, do you feel, were the excuses the neighbor offered?

7. English translations of the Bible generally make it difficult, even impossible, for us to understand the point of the parable.

    a. Jesus' opening statement, "Suppose one of you," must be understood to say, "Can you imagine anything like this [the story that follows] ever happening?" His hearers would then respond, "Never! Impossible!"

    b. The word translated as "importunity" or "persistence" in 11:8 (understood to refer to the would-be host) should be translated as "sense of shame," and points to the fact that the neighbor will go to great lengths to preserve his reputation in the community.

    When these two points are kept in mind, how do they help us understand the point of Jesus' story?

8. What exhortation does Jesus make in 11:9, and what assurance does he give in 11:10?

9. What is the meaning of 11:11,12?

10. Compare 11:13 with Matthew 7:11. According to Luke, what are the "good gifts" Jesus refers to in Matthew 7:11?

11. Summarize briefly the message that Luke 11:9–13 speaks to us today.

Read Luke 12:13–21

---

1. A man comes to Jesus with a request for help, 12:13. What was his problem, and what action did he want Jesus to take to help him solve it?

2. How did Jesus respond to his request, 12:14,15?

3. What challenge confronted the rich man in Jesus' parable, 12:16,17?

4. What solution did he choose, 12:18?

5. Whom did he consult in making his decision?

6. What goal did he have in making his decision, 12:19?

7. There is a fatal flaw in the rich man's thinking. What is it, 12:20?

8. Though the rich man was concerned about where he might place his abundance, what might he have done with it?

9. Ambrose, an early church father, said there was plenty of room for the rich man's surplus supplies—in the mouths of the poor. How do you respond to Ambrose's statement?

10. What is the meaning of 12:21?

11. What powerful message does the parable speak to each of us in today's world?

Read Luke 14:15–24

---

1. Read Luke 14:1–14. What was the context in which Jesus told this parable?

2. What is the meaning of the statement the speaker made in 14:15?

3. Two invitations were issued for this banquet: an initial one, and a second one when the food was ready. Why were two invitations needed?

4. What excuse did the first person offer, and why was it invalid, 14:18?

5. What excuse did the second person offer, and why was it invalid, 14:19?

6. What excuse did the third person offer, and why was it invalid, 14:20?

7. Why might those first invited have declined?

8. The host sent his servant out again to invite others previously not invited, 14:21.

   a. Note that a rich host would normally not invite a poor person to a banquet. Why not?

   b. What connection do you see between the disabilities of those invited later and the three excuses of those invited earlier?

9. The host sent his servant out a third time to invite even more people to his banquet, 14:22,23.

   a. Why would he have wanted as many as possible to attend?

   b. Why would it have been necessary for the servant to "compel" those now invited to attend?

10. The point of the parable is timeless.

    a. What message did the parable speak to Jesus' hearers?

    b. What message does it speak to us today?

Read Luke 15:1–10

---

1. What prompted Jesus to tell the trio of parables in Luke 15? See 15:1,2.

2. Why would the Pharisees and scribes have been angry with Jesus?

3. When people in the Western world share a meal, they view the event as a happy occasion that meets a need and provides some fellowship. In Jesus' day, what did eating together imply for those who shared a meal?

4. The shepherd would have had to expend a lot of energy in lifting the sheep onto his shoulders and carrying it back to his village community. What light does this throw on the "cost" of God's saving work in Jesus?

5. In Jesus' day, some rabbis affirmed that they were indeed "completely righteous" persons whom God loved in a special way. Some taught that "as for the perfectly righteous [*who never sinned at all*], 'the eye hath not seen, O God, beside thee, what he hath prepared for him that waiteth for him.'" Other rabbis said that God's greatest love was extended to repentant sinners. What was Jesus' attitude toward these opinions?

6. The woman seeking her lost coin would have been more certain of finding it than was the shepherd who set out to find the lost sheep. Why?

7. Jesus took a certain risk in making a woman the heroine in a parable, especially when telling it to scribes and Pharisees. Why?

8. Some people ask, "Have you found the Lord?" In light of the parables of the Lost Sheep and the Lost Coin, how might the question be reworded to more accurately reflect biblical teaching concerning salvation?

9. When the shepherd returned to his village with the lost sheep across his shoulders, everyone would have rejoiced. When the woman found her coin, she invited others in the village to rejoice with her. What does this say about how churches should feel toward those in their communities who are without Christ?

10. Why have some Christians and some churches lost their passion for reaching the lost? What might they do to remedy this?

Read Luke 15:11–32

---

1. A Pharisaic commentary on the Law said, "There is joy before God when those who provoke him perish from the world." Compare this statement with 15:7 and 15:10.

2. When the younger son asked the father to give him the share of the property that belonged to him, what was he really saying to his father?

3. When the younger son made his request to his father, the older brother should have immediately undertaken the role of an intermediary between his brother and father. Why might he not have wanted to do that?

4. When the younger brother departed, he literally "went away from his own people." Why would that have been a very risky thing to do in the society of his day?

5. How do you think the father felt when he saw his son walk away, and while his son was away? What does this teach us about "the heart of God"?

6. Why might the citizen in the far country have offered the younger son a job feeding *pigs*?

7. When the younger son "came to himself," what prompted that—repentance, or a sense of physical need?

8. The younger son, in working out what to say to his father when he returned to his village, decided to ask for help in learning a trade. Why?

9. In the world of Jesus' day, it was considered very inappropriate for old men to run. Why, then, did the father run toward his son when he recognized him?

10. Why didn't the younger son ask his father to treat him like one of his hired hands?

11. After the son's return, the father ordered his servants to prepare a feast to which all the village would have been invited. At this feast, the father would have been the central figure and the younger son the guest of honor. The older brother would have been expected to welcome all guests to the family home, take them to his father, and serve as "head waiter." He would have been responsible for supervising those serving the meal. What light do these factors throw on the older brother's behavior?

12. We are not told how the older brother eventually responded to his father's pleas to join the festivities.

    a. What might he have done?

    b. What did the Pharisees finally do to Jesus, who received and ate with sinners?

    c. What questions does this parable pose for each of us?

Read Luke 16:1–8

Note: The most probable cultural setting for the parable is that of a landed estate with a manager who had authority to carry out the business of the estate for its owner, referred to as the "master" in the text. The master was a man of noble character, respected in the community, who cared enough about his wealth to fire a wasteful manager. The debtors were most likely renters who agreed to pay a fixed amount of produce for the yearly rent. The manager was a salaried official, who, in addition, was paid a specific fee by the renter for each contract. He was no doubt making a few extras "under the table," but these amounts were not reflected in the signed bills and were not necessarily exorbitant.

1. When the master fired the manager, the latter remained silent. Why might he have chosen to remain silent?

2. When the manager found himself out of a job, his future survival was at stake.

    a. Why did he reject the idea of earning a living by digging or begging?

    b. What scheme did he come up with, 16:4?

3. To ingratiate himself with his "victims," he had to place them under obligation. How did he achieve this?

4. Why would the manager have had to act quickly and decisively to achieve his goal?

5. News of the master's so-called "generosity" would have spread around the village like wildfire. Why?

6. The master found himself trapped by the manager's actions. Why?

7. What two courses of action might the master have taken to resolve the situation?

8. We are told that the master "commended" the unjust manager. For what did he commend him?

9. What is the meaning of 16:9?

10. What light does Matthew 25:36–40 throw on how we might make eternal "friends" for ourselves through our use of money?

Read Luke 18:1–8

---

1. Why did Jesus tell this parable?

2. The parable refers to a judge. According to the parable, what kind of disposition did he have?

3. What do the following passages say about the attitude Israelite society was to adopt toward widows?

    a. Exodus 22:22–23

    b. Deuteronomy 10:18

    c. Deuteronomy 24:17

    d. Deuteronomy 27:19

    e. Job 22:9

    f. Job 24:3,21

    g. Psalm 68:5

    h. Isaiah 1:17,23

    i. Isaiah 10:2

4. Jewish legal tradition required that the suit of an orphan must always be heard first, and that of a widow next. What do the following passages say about the behavior of some of ancient Israel's rulers and judges?

    a. Micah 3

    b. Amos 2:6,7

    c. Amos 5:10–13

    d. 2 Chronicles 19:4–6

5. Why did the judge finally give the widow a hearing?

6. What is the message of the parable to us today? Note verses 7 and 8 as you ponder this question.

Read Luke 18:9–14

---

1. According to 18:9, why did Jesus tell this parable?

2. Compare the length of the Pharisee's prayer with the length of the prayer the tax collector offered. What does the comparison reveal?

3. When the Pharisee prayed, he kept himself separate from others. Why?

4. When the tax collector prayed, he also kept himself separate from others. Why?

5. Without doubt, when the Pharisee prayed, he prayed to be heard by those around him. Why?

6. What was the content of the Pharisee's prayer?

7. What was the content of the tax collector's prayer?

8. When the Pharisee prayed, his concern was to tell God what he had done for Him. When the tax collector prayed, his concern was what God might do for him. Only the tax collector went home justified.

   a. What might we learn from this to improve our personal prayer life?

   b. Why is it more important to *listen to God* than to *tell God* all about ourselves?

NOTES